GREEK TRAGEDIES

VOLUME 3

AESCHYLUS
The Eumenides Translated by Richmond Lattimore

SOPHOCLES
Philoctetes Translated by David Grene
Oedipus at Colonus Translated by Robert Fitzgerald

EURIPIDES
The Bacchae Translated by William Arrowsmith
Alcestis Translated by Richmond Lattimore

Edited by David Grene & Richmond Lattimore

THIRD EDITION *Edited by Mark Griffith & Glenn W. Most*

GREEK TRAGEDIES

VOLUME 3

The University of Chicago Press CHICAGO & LONDON

MARK GRIFFITH is professor of classics and
of theater, dance, and performance studies at
the University of California, Berkeley.

GLENN W. MOST is professor of ancient
Greek at the Scuola Normale Superiore at Pisa
and a visiting member of the Committee on
Social Thought at the University of Chicago.

DAVID GRENE (1913–2002) taught classics for
many years at the University of Chicago.

RICHMOND LATTIMORE (1906–1984),
professor of Greek at Bryn Mawr College,
was a poet and translator best known for his
translations of the Greek classics, especially his
versions of the *Iliad* and the *Odyssey*.

The University of Chicago Press, Chicago 60637
The University of Chicago Press, Ltd., London
© 2013 by The University of Chicago

The Eumenides © 1953, 2013 by the University
of Chicago
Philoctetes © 1957, 2013 by the University of
Chicago
Oedipus at Colonus from Sophocles: *The Oedipus
Cycle*, translated by Dudley Fitts and Robert
Fitzgerald. © 1941 by Houghton Mifflin
Harcourt Publishing Company. Copyright
renewed 1969 by Robert Fitzgerald. Reprinted
by permission of Houghton Mifflin Harcourt
Publishing Company
The Bacchae © 1959, 2013 by the University of
Chicago
Alcestis © 1955, 2013 by the University of
Chicago

22 21 20 19 18 17 16 15 14 13   1 2 3 4 5

ISBN-13: 978-0-226-03576-5 (cloth)
ISBN-13: 978-0-226-03593-2 (paper)
ISBN-13: 978-0-226-03609-0 (e-book)

Library of Congress Cataloging-in-Publication
Data

Greek tragedies / edited by David Grene and
Richmond Lattimore. — Third edition / edited
by Mark Griffith and Glenn W. Most.
   pages. cm.
   ISBN 978-0-226-03514-7 (cloth : alk. paper)
— ISBN 978-0-226-03528-4 (pbk. : alk. paper)
— ISBN 978-0-226-03531-4 (e-book) — ISBN
978-0-226-03545-1 (cloth : alk. paper) — ISBN
978-0-226-03559-8 (pbk. : alk. paper) — ISBN 978-
0-226-03562-8 (e-book) — ISBN 978-0-226-
03576-5 (cloth : alk. paper) — ISBN 978-0-
226-03593-2 (pbk. : alk. paper) — ISBN 978-0-
226-03609-0 (e-book) 1. Greek drama (Tragedy)
I. Grene, David. II. Lattimore, Richmond,
1906–1984. III. Wyckoff, Elizabeth, 1915– IV.
Most, Glenn W. V. Griffith, Mark (Classicist)
VI. Sophocles. Antigone. English. 2013. VII.
Sophocles. Oedipus Rex. English. 2013. VIII.
Aeschylus. Agamemnon. English. 2013. IX.
Aeschylus. Prometheus bound. English. 2013. X.
Euripides. Hippolytus. English. 2013.
   PA3626.A2G57 2013
   882'.0108—dc23
                                    2012044399

CONTENTS

THE EUMENIDES

AESCHYLUS
Translated by Richmond Lattimore

INTRODUCTION TO AESCHYLUS' THE EUMENIDES

The Eumenides was presented in 458 BCE as the last tragedy in the trilogy called the *Oresteia*. The other plays in the trilogy are *Agamemnon* and *The Libation Bearers*. Each of the three can be studied and interpreted as an independent drama, in isolation from the other two.

When Orestes murdered his mother, he did so at the command of Apollo, but even Apollo could not by formal absolution drive away her Furies (ultimately canonized as the Eumenides), who pursued the murderer up and down the world. At last the case was brought to Athens and tried by law, before a jury of Athenian citizens, with Athena presiding as judge (and also participating in the voting), the Furies acting as prosecutors, and Apollo as counsel for the defense. Athena (who was born without a mother) voted in favor of the father, and Orestes was acquitted by the narrowest of margins. She then appeased the angry Furies (Eumenides) by establishing a cult for them near the Acropolis, as guardian spirits of Athens.

As a drama of atonement, absolution, and canonization, *The Eumenides* bears some resemblance to Sophocles' *Oedipus at Colonus*. In both cases the hero, who feels himself to be morally blameless, is nevertheless contaminated by horrendous past actions and must be absolved. But Sophocles keeps his supernatural powers in the background. Aeschylus stages his; and his issues are public, not individual, as the story of the Argive House of Atreus in its rescue from recurrent bloodshed and revenge merges into the history of civilization at Athens.

THE EUMENIDES

Characters THE PYTHIAN PRIESTESS OF APOLLO
APOLLO
HERMES (silent character)
ORESTES, son of Agamemnon
GHOST of Clytaemestra
CHORUS of Furies (Eumenides)
ATHENA
JURYMEN (silent)
SECOND CHORUS, women of Athens

Scene: For the first part of the play (1–234) the scene is Delphi, in front of the sanctuary of Pythian Apollo. The action of the rest of the play (235 to the end) takes place at Athens, on the Acropolis in front of the temple of Athena.

(Enter the Pythian Priestess, from the side.)

PYTHIA
    I give first place of honor in my prayer to her
    who of the gods first prophesied, the Earth; and next
    to Themis, who succeeded to her mother's place
    of prophecy; so runs the legend; and in third
    succession, given by free consent, not won by force,   5
    another Titan daughter of Earth was seated here.
    This was Phoebe. She gave it as a birthday gift
    to Phoebus, who is called still after Phoebe's name.
    And he, leaving the pond of Delos and the reef,
    grounded his ship at the roadstead of Pallas, then   10

made his way to this land and a Parnassian home.
Deep in respect for his degree Hephaestus' sons
conveyed him here, for these are builders of roads, and
    changed
the wilderness to a land that was no wilderness.
He came so, and the people highly honored him,   15
with Delphus, lord and helmsman of the country. Zeus
made his mind full with godship and prophetic craft
and placed him, fourth in a line of seers, upon this throne.
So, Loxias is the spokesman of his father, Zeus.
These are the gods I set in the proem of my prayer.   20
But Pallas-before-the-temple has her right in all
I say. I worship the nymphs where the Corycian rock
is hollowed inward, haunt of birds and paced by gods.
Bromius, whom I forget not, sways this place. From here
in divine form he led his Bacchanals in arms   25
to hunt down Pentheus like a hare in the deathtrap.
I call upon the springs of Pleistus, on the power
of Poseidon, and on final loftiest Zeus,
then go to sit in prophecy on the throne. May all
grant me that this of all my entrances shall be   30
the best by far. If there are any Hellenes here
let them draw lots, so enter, as the custom is.
My prophecy is only as the god may guide.

> *(She enters the temple and almost immediately*
> *comes out again, crawling on all fours.)*

Things terrible to tell and for the eyes to see
terrible drove me out again from Loxias' house   35
so that I have no strength and cannot stand on springing
feet, but run with hands' help and my legs have no speed.
An old woman afraid is nothing: a child, no more.
See, I am on my way to the wreath-hung recess
and on the centerstone I see a man with god's   40
defilement on him postured in the suppliant's seat

with blood dripping from his hands and from a new-drawn
    sword,
holding too a branch that had grown high on an olive
tree, decorously wrapped in a great tuft of wool,
and the fleece shone. So far, at least, I can speak clear.   45
In front of this man slept a startling company
of women lying all upon the chairs. Or not
women, I think I call them rather Gorgons, only
not Gorgons either, since their shape is not the same.
I saw some creatures painted in a picture once,   50
who tore the food from Phineus, only these have no
wings, that could be seen; they are black and utterly
repulsive, and they snore with breath that drives one back.
From their eyes drips the foul ooze, and their dress is such
as is not right to wear in the presence of the gods'   55
statues, nor even in any human house.
I have never seen the tribe that spawned this company
nor know what piece of earth can claim with pride it bore
such brood, and without hurt and tears for labor given.
    Now after this the master of the house must take   60
his own measures: Apollo Loxias, who is very strong
and heals by divination, reads portentous signs,
and so purifies the houses others hold as well.

(Exit the Pythia. The doors of the temple open and show Orestes
surrounded by the sleeping Furies, Apollo and Hermes beside him.)

APOLLO

I will not give you up. Through to the end standing
your guardian, whether by your side or far away,   65
I shall not weaken toward your enemies. See now
how I have caught and overpowered these rabid creatures.
The repulsive maidens have been stilled to sleep, those gray
and aged children, they with whom no mortal man,
no god, nor even any beast, will have to do.   70
It was because of evil they were born, because

they hold the evil darkness of the Pit below
earth, loathed alike by men and by the heavenly gods.
Nevertheless, run from them, never weaken. They
will chase your track as you stride on across the long   75
land, and your driven feet forever pound the earth,
on across the main water and the circle-washed
cities. Be herdsman to this hard march. Never fail
until you come at last to Pallas' citadel.
Kneel there, and clasp the ancient idol in your arms,   80
and there we shall find those who will judge this case, and
     words
to say that will have magic in their figures. Thus
you will be rid of your afflictions, once for all.
For it was I who made you strike your mother down.

ORESTES

My lord Apollo, you understand what it means to do   85
no wrong. Learn also what it is not to neglect.
None can mistrust your power to do good, if you will.°

APOLLO

Remember: let not the fear overcome your heart.
Hermes, you are my brother from a single sire.
Look after him, and as you are named the god who guides,   90
be such in strong fact. He is my suppliant. Shepherd him
with fortunate escort on his journeys among men.
The wanderer has rights which Zeus acknowledges.

> (Exit Apollo into the temple, Orestes guided by Hermes
> to the side. Enter the Ghost of Clytaemestra.)

CLYTAEMESTRA

You would sleep, then? And what use are you, if you sleep?
It is because of you I go dishonored thus   95
among the rest of the dead. Because of those I killed
reproaches among the perished never cease for me
and I am driven in disgrace. I say to you

that I am charged with guilt most grave by these. And yet
I suffered too, horribly, and from those most dear,   100
yet none among the powers is angered for my sake
that I was slaughtered, and by matricidal hands.
Look at these gashes in my heart, think where they came
from. Eyes illuminate the sleeping brain,
but in the daylight man's future cannot be seen.°   105
Yet I have given you much to lap up, outpourings
without wine, sober propitiations, sacrificed
in secrecy of night and on a hearth of fire
for you, at an hour given to no other god.
Now I watch all these honors trampled into the ground,   110
and he is out and gone away like a hunted fawn
so lightly, from the very middle of your nets,
sprung clear, and laughing merrily at you. Hear me.
It is my life depends upon this spoken plea.
Think then, O goddesses beneath the ground. For I,   115
the dream of Clytaemestra, call upon your name.

(The Furies stir in their sleep and whimper.)

CLYTAEMESTRA

Oh, whimper, then, but your man has got away and gone
far. He has friends to help him, who are not like mine.   120

(They whimper again.)

CLYTAEMESTRA

Too much sleep and no pity for my plight. I stand,
his mother, here, killed by Orestes. He is gone.

(They moan in their sleep.)

CLYTAEMESTRA

You moan, you sleep. Get on your feet quickly, will you?
What have you yet got done, except to do evil?   125

(They moan again.)

CLYTAEMESTRA

Sleep and fatigue, two masterful conspirators,
have dimmed the deadly anger of the mother-snake.

(The Chorus start violently, then cry out in their sleep.)

CHORUS [*singing*]

Get him, get him, get him, get him! Make sure!　　　　　　130

CLYTAEMESTRA

The beast you are after is a dream, but like the hound
whose thought of hunting has no lapse, you bay him on.
What are you about? Up, let not work's weariness
beat you, nor slacken with sleep so you forget my pain.
Scold your own heart and hurt it, as it well deserves,　　　135
for this is discipline's spur upon her own. Let go
upon this man the stormblasts of your bloodshot breath,
wither him in your wind, after him, hunt him down
once more, and shrivel him in your stomach's heat and flame.

*(Exit the Ghost. The Chorus begin to waken and
enter from the temple, one by one.)*

CHORUS LEADER

Waken. You are awake, wake her, as I did you.　　　　　140
You dream still? On your feet and kick your sleep aside.
Let us see whether this prelude was in vain.

CHORUS [*singing*]

STROPHE A

Sisters, we have had wrong done us.
When I have undergone so much and all in vain.
Suffering, suffering, bitter, oh shame shame,　　　　　145
unendurable wrong.
The hunted beast has slipped clean from our nets and gone.
Sleep defeated me, and I lost my prey.

ANTISTROPHE A

Shame, son of Zeus! Robber is all you are.
A young god, you have ridden down powers gray with age,　　150

honored the suppliant, though a godless man, who hurt
the mother who gave him birth.
Yourself a god, you stole the matricide away.
Where in this act shall any man say there is right?

STROPHE B

The accusation came upon me from my dreams,   155
and hit me, as with a goad in the midgrip of his fist
the charioteer strikes,
but deep, beneath lobe and heart.
The public scourger's cutting whip is mine to feel   160
and the weight of pain is big, heavy to bear.

ANTISTROPHE B

Such are the actions of the younger gods. These occupy
by unconditional force, beyond all right, a throne
that runs reeking blood,
blood at the feet, blood at the head.   165
The very stone center of earth here in our eyes horrible
with blood and curse stands plain to see.

STROPHE C

Himself a seer, he has spoiled his secret shrine's
hearth with the stain, driven and hallooed the action on.   170
He made man's way cross the place of the ways of god
and blighted age-old distributions of power.

ANTISTROPHE C

He has wounded me, but he shall not get this man away.
Let him hide under the ground, he shall never go free.   175
Cursed suppliant, he shall feel against his head
another murderer rising out of the same seed.

(Enter Apollo again, from his sanctuary.)

APOLLO

Get out, I tell you, go and leave this house. Away
in haste, from your presence set the mantic chamber free,   180
else you may feel the flash and bite of a flying snake

launched from the twisted thong of gold that spans my bow
to make you in your pain spew out the black and foaming
blood of men, vomit the clots sucked from their veins.
This house is no right place for such as you to cling   185
upon; but where, by judgment given, heads are lopped
and eyes gouged out, throats cut, and by destruction of seed
the potency of boys is ruined,° where mutilation
lives, and stoning, and the long moan of tortured men
spiked underneath the spine and fixed on stakes. Listen   190
to how the gods spit out the manner of that feast
your appetites prefer. The whole way you look is guide
to what you are—the likes of whom should hole in the cave
of the blood-reeking lion, not wipe off your filth
on others nearby, in this oracular sanctuary.   195
Out then, you flock of goats without a herdsman, since
no god has such affection as to tend this herd.

CHORUS LEADER
My lord Apollo, it is your turn to listen now.
Your own part in this is more than accessory.
You are the one who did it; all the guilt is yours.   200

APOLLO
So? How? Continue speaking, until I understand.

CHORUS LEADER
You gave this outlander the word to kill his mother.

APOLLO
The word to exact price for his father. What of that?

CHORUS LEADER
You then dared take him in, fresh from his bloodletting.

APOLLO
Yes, and I told him to take refuge in this house.   205

CHORUS LEADER
Yet you abuse us, after we escorted him here?

APOLLO

Yes. It was not for you to come near this house.

CHORUS LEADER

And yet we have our duty—to do what we have done.

APOLLO

An office? You? Sound forth your glorious privilege.

CHORUS LEADER

This: to drive matricides out of their houses.   210

APOLLO

                                        Then
what if it be the woman and she kills her husband?

CHORUS LEADER

Such murder would not be the shedding of kindred blood.

APOLLO

You have made into a thing of no account, no place,
the sworn faith of Zeus and of Hera, lady
of consummations, and Cypris by such argument   215
is thrown away, outlawed, and yet the sweetest things
in man's life come from her, for married love between
man and woman is bigger than oaths, guarded by right
of nature. If when such kill each other you are slack
so as not to take vengeance nor eye them in wrath,   220
then I deny your manhunt of Orestes goes
with right. I see that one cause moves you to strong rage
but on the other clearly you are unmoved to act.
Pallas divine shall review the pleadings of this case.

CHORUS LEADER

Nothing will ever make me let that man go free.   225

APOLLO

Keep after him then, and make more trouble for yourselves.

CHORUS LEADER

Do not try to curtail my privilege by argument.

APOLLO

I would not take your privilege if you gave it me.

CHORUS LEADER

No, for you are called great beside the throne of Zeus
already, but the motherblood drives me, and I go   230
to win my right upon this man and hunt him down.

APOLLO

But I shall give this suppliant help and rescue, for
if I willingly fail him who turns to me for aid,
his wrath, before gods and men, is a fearful thing.

*(Exit all separately. The scene is now Athens, on the Acropolis in
front of the temple and statue of Athena. Enter Orestes from the
side. He takes up a suppliant posture at the feet of the statue.)*

ORESTES

My lady Athena, it is at Loxias' behest   235
I come. So take in of your grace the wanderer
who comes, no suppliant, not unwashed of hand, but one
blunted at last, and worn and battered on the outland
habitations and the journeyings of men.
Crossing the dry land and the sea alike, keeping   240
the ordinances of Apollo's oracle
I come, goddess, before your statue and your house
to keep watch here and wait the issue of my trial.

(Enter the Chorus from the side.)

CHORUS LEADER

So. Here the man has left a clear trail behind; keep on,   245
keep on, as the unspeaking accuser tells us, by
whose sense, like hounds after a bleeding fawn, we trail
our quarry by the splash and drip of blood. And now
my lungs are blown with abundant and with wearisome
work, mankilling. My range has been the entire extent
of land, and, flown unwinged across the open water,   250

I am here, and give way to no ship in my pursuit.
Our man has gone to cover somewhere in this place.
The welcome smell of human blood has told me so.

CHORUS [*singing*]
  Look again, look again,
  search everywhere, let   255
  not the matricide
  steal away and escape.

                                        (*They see Orestes.*)

  See there! He clings to defense
  again, his arms winding the immortal goddess'
  image, so seeks acquittal out of our hands.   260
  It shall not be. His mother's blood spilled on the ground
  cannot come back again.
  It is all soaked and drained into the ground and gone.

  You must give back for her blood from the living man
  red blood of your body to suck, and from your own   265
  I could feed, with bitter-swallowed drench,
  turn your strength limp while yet you live and drag you down
  where you must pay for the pain of the murdered mother,
  and watch the rest of the mortals stained with violence
  against god or guest   270
  or hurt parents who were close and dear,
  each with the pain upon him that his crime deserves.
  Hades is great, Hades calls men to reckoning
  there under the ground,
  sees all, and inscribes it deep in his recording mind. 275

ORESTES
  I have been beaten and been taught, I understand
  the many rules of absolution, where it is right
  to speak and where be silent. In this action now
  speech has been ordered by my teacher, who is wise.
  The stain of blood dulls now and fades upon my hand.   280

My blot of matricide is being washed away.
When it was fresh still, at the hearth of the god, Phoebus,
it was absolved and driven out by sacrifice
of a pig, and the list were long if I went back to tell
of all I met who were not hurt by being with me.   285
Time in his aging overtakes all things alike.
Now it is from pure mouth and with good auspices
I call upon Athena, queen of this land, to come
and rescue me. She, without work of her spear, shall win
myself and all my land and all the Argive host   290
to stand her staunch companion for the rest of time.
Whether now ranging somewhere in the Libyan land
beside her father's crossing and by Triton's run
of waters she sets her foot upright or enshrouded
rescuing there her friends, or on the Phlegraean plain   295
like some bold man of armies sweeps with eyes the scene,
let her come! She is a god and hears me far away.
So may she set me free from what is at my back.

CHORUS LEADER

Neither Apollo nor Athena's strength can win
you free, save you from going down forgotten, without   300
knowing where joy lies anywhere inside your heart,
blood drained, chewed dry by the powers of death, a wraith,
    a shell.
You will not speak to answer, spew my challenge away?
You are consecrate to me and fattened for my feast,
and you shall feed me while you live, not cut down first   305
at the altar. Hear the spell I sing to bind you in.

CHORUS [chanting]

Come then, link we our choral dance.
Ours to show forth the power
and terror of our music, declare
our rights of office, how we conspire   310
to steer men's lives.
We hold we are straight and just. If a man

can spread his hands and show they are clean,
no wrath of ours shall lurk for him.
Unscathed he walks through his life time.   315
But one like this man before us, with stained
hidden hands, and the guilt upon him,
shall find us beside him, as witnesses
of the truth, and we show clear in the end
to avenge the blood of the murdered.   320

[*singing*]

STROPHE A

Mother, O my mother night, who gave me
birth, to be a vengeance on the seeing
and the blind, hear me. For Leto's
youngling takes my right away,
stealing from my clutch the prey   325
that cowers, whose blood would wipe
at last the motherblood away.

REFRAIN A

Over the beast doomed to the fire
this is the chant, scatter of wits,
frenzy and fear, hurting the heart,   330
song of the Furies
binding brain and blighting blood
in its stringless melody.

ANTISTROPHE A

This the purpose that all-involving
Destiny spun, to be ours and to be shaken   335
never: when mortals assume outrage
of their own hand in violence,
these we hound, till one goes
under earth. Nor does death
set them altogether free.   340

REFRAIN A

Over the beast doomed to the fire

this is the chant, scatter of wits,
frenzy and fear, hurting the heart,
song of the Furies
binding brain and blighting blood   345
in its stringless melody.

When we were born such lots were assigned for our keeping.
So the immortals must hold hands off, nor is there   350
one of them who shall sit at our feasting.
In pure white robes I have no interest and no portion.°

I have chosen overthrow
of houses, where the battle god   355
grown within strikes near and dear
down. So we swoop upon this man
here. He is strong, but we wear him down
for the blood that is still wet on him.

Being eager to save all others from these concerns   360
by our efforts we provide for the gods immunity,°
and no appeal comes to them,
since Zeus has ruled our blood-dripping company   365
outcast, nor will deal with us.

I have chosen overthrow
of houses, where the battle god
grown within strikes near and dear
down. So we swoop upon this man
here. He is strong, but we wear him down
for the blood that is still wet on him.

Men's illusions in their pride under the sky melt
down, and are diminished into the ground, gone

before the onset of our black robes, and the dancing   370
of our vindictive feet against them.

For with a long leap from high
above and dead drop of weight
I bring foot's force crashing down
to cut the legs from under even   375
the runner, and spill him to ruin.

He falls, and does not know in the daze of his folly.
Such in the dark of man is the mist of infection
that hovers, and moaning rumor tells how his house lies
under fog that glooms above.   380

For with a long leap from high
above, and dead drop of weight,
I bring foot's force crashing down
to cut the legs from under even
the runner, and spill him to ruin.

All holds.° For we are strong and skilled;
we have authority; we hold
memory of evil; we are stern,
nor can men's pleadings bend us. We
accomplish our duties, spurned, outcast   385
from gods, standing apart in slime
unlit by the sun. Rocky and rough are the paths
for those who see and alike for those whose eyes are lost.

Is there a man who does not fear
this, does not shrink to hear   390
how my place has been ordained,
granted and given by destiny

and the gods, absolute? Privilege
primeval yet is mine, nor am I without place
though it be underneath the ground 395
and in no sunlight and in darkness that I must stand.

(Enter Athena, in full armor.)

ATHENA

From far away I heard the outcry of your call.
It was beside Scamandrus. I was taking claim
of land, for there the Achaean lords of war and first
fighters gave me large portion of all their spears 400
had won, the land root and stock to be mine for all
eternity, for the sons of Theseus a choice gift.
From there, sped on my weariless feet, I came, wingless
but in the rush and speed of the aegis fold.° And now
I see upon this land a strange new company 405
which, though it brings no terror to my eyes, brings still
wonder. Who are you? I address you all alike,
both you, the stranger kneeling at my image here,
and you, who are like no seed ever begotten, not 410
recognized by the gods as goddesses, nor yet
stamped in the likenesses of any human form.
But no. This is the place of the just. Its rights forbid
to speak evil of another who is without blame.

CHORUS LEADER

Daughter of Zeus, you shall hear all compressed to brief 415
measure. We are the eternal children of the Night.
Curses they call us in our homes beneath the ground.

ATHENA

I know your race, then, and the names by which you are
called.

CHORUS LEADER

And soon you shall be told of our prerogatives.

ATHENA

I can know them, if someone will give me a clear account.   420

CHORUS LEADER

We drive from home those who have shed the blood of men.

ATHENA

Where is the place, then, where the killer's flight shall end?

CHORUS LEADER

A place where happiness is nevermore allowed.

ATHENA

Is he one? Do you blast him to this kind of flight?

CHORUS LEADER

Yes. He murdered his mother by deliberate choice.   425

ATHENA

Not by compulsion, nor fear of someone's wrath?

CHORUS LEADER

Where is the spur to justify man's matricide?

ATHENA

Here are two sides, and only half the argument.

CHORUS LEADER

He is unwilling to give or to accept an oath.

ATHENA

You wish to be called righteous rather than act right.   430

CHORUS LEADER

No. How so? From the wealth of your wisdom, explain.

ATHENA

I say, wrong must not win merely by oaths.

CHORUS LEADER

Examine him then yourself. Decide it, and be fair.

ATHENA

You would turn over authority in this case to me?

CHORUS LEADER

By all means. We respect your merits and whence they are
    derived.°   435

ATHENA

Your turn, stranger. What will you say in answer? Speak,
tell me your country and your birth, what has befallen
you, then defend yourself against the censure of these;
if it is confidence in the right that makes you sit
guarding this image near my hearth, a suppliant   440
in the tradition of Ixion, sacrosanct.
Give me an answer which is plain to understand.

ORESTES

Lady Athena, first I will take the great worry
away that lies in these last words you spoke. I am
no suppliant, nor was it because I had a stain   445
upon my hand that I sat at your image. I
will give you a strong proof that what I say is true.
It is the law that the man of the bloody hand must speak
no word until, by action of an expert purifier,
the slaughter of a young animal has washed his blood away. 450
Long since, at the homes of others, I have been absolved
thus, both by running waters and by victims slain.
I count this scruple now out of the way. Learn next
with no delay where I am from. I am of Argos
and it is to my honor that you ask the name   455
of my father, Agamemnon, lord of seafarers,
and your companion when you made the Trojan city
of Ilium no city any more. He died
without honor when he came home. It was my mother
of the dark heart, who entangled him in intricate nets   460
and cut him down. The bath is witness to his death.
I was an exile in the time before this. I came back

and killed the woman who gave me birth. I don't deny it.
My father was dear, and this was vengeance for his blood.
Apollo shares responsibility for this.   465
He counterspurred my heart and told me of pains to come
if I should fail to act against the guilty ones.
This is my case. Decide if it be right or wrong.
I am in your hands. Where my fate falls, I shall accept.

ATHENA

The matter is too big for any mortal man   470
who thinks he can judge it. Nor yet do I have the right
to analyse cases of murder where wrath's edge
is sharp, and all the more since you have come, and clung
a clean and innocent suppliant against my doors.
You bring no harm to my city. I respect your rights.   475
Yet these, too, have their work. We cannot brush them aside,
and if this action so runs that they fail to win,
the venom of their resolution will return
to infect the soil, and sicken all my land to death.
Here is dilemma. Whether I let them stay or drive   480
them off, it is a hard course and will hurt. So, since
the burden of the case is here, and rests on me,
I shall select judges of manslaughter, and swear
them in, establish a court into all time to come.
Litigants, call your witnesses, have ready your proofs   485
as evidence under bond to keep this case secure.
I will pick the finest of my citizens, and come
back. They shall swear to make no judgment that is not
just, and make clear where in this action the truth lies.

(Exit Athena, to the side.)

CHORUS [singing]

STROPHE A

Here is overthrow of all   490
established laws,° if the claim
of this matricide shall stand

good, his crime be sustained.
Should this be, every man will find a way
to act at his own caprice;   495
over and over again in time
to come, parents shall await
the deathstroke at their children's hands.

We are the Angry Ones. But we
shall watch no more over works   500
of men, and so act. We shall
let loose indiscriminate death.
Man shall learn from man's lot, forejudge
the evils of his neighbor's case,
seek respite and escape from troubles:
pathetic prophet who consoles   505
with strengthless cures, in vain.

Nevermore let one who feels
the stroke of accident, uplift
his voice and make outcry, thus: 510
"Oh Justice!
Throned powers of the Furies, help!"
Such might be the pitiful cry
of some father, of the stricken
mother, their appeal. Now   515
the House of Justice has collapsed.

There are times when fear is good.
It must keep its watchful place
at the heart's controls. There is
advantage   520
in the wisdom won from pain.
If the city, if the man
rears a heart that nowhere goes

in fear, how shall such a one
any more respect the right?   525

Refuse the life of anarchy;
refuse the life devoted to
one master.
The in-between has the power
by a god's grant always, though   530
his ordinances vary.
I will speak in defense
of reason: for the very child
of vanity is Violence;
but out of health   535
in the heart is born the beloved
and the longed-for, prosperity.

All for all I tell you: show
respect for the altar of right.
You shall not   540
eye advantage, and kick
it over with foot of force.
Vengeance will be upon you.
The appointed end awaits.
Let someone see this and take   545
care, to mother and father,
and to the guest
in the gates welcomed, give all honor,
respecting their position.

The man who does right, free-willed, without constraint   550
shall not lose happiness
nor be wiped out with all his generation.
But the transgressor, I tell you, the bold man
who heaps up confusion of goods unjustly won,

at long last and perforce, when his ship toils   555
in the storm must strike his sail
midst the wreck of his rigging.

He calls on those who hear not, caught inside
the hard wrestle of water.
The divinity laughs at the hot-hearted man,   560
the man who said "never to me," watches him
pinned in distress, unable to run free of the wave crests.
He had good luck in his life. Now
he smashes on the reef of right
and drowns, unwept and forgotten.   565

(Athena reenters from the side, guiding eleven citizens
chosen as jurors° and attended by a herald.)

ATHENA

Herald, make proclamation and gather in the host
assembled. Let the stabbing voice of the Etruscan
trumpet, blown to the full with mortal wind, crash out
its high call to all the mustered populace.
For in the filling of this deliberative assembly   570
it is best for all the city to be silent and learn
the measures I have laid down into the rest of time.
So too these litigants, that their case be fairly tried.

(Trumpet call. All take their places. Enter Apollo.)

CHORUS LEADER

My lord Apollo, rule within your own domain.
What in this matter has to do with you? Declare.   575

APOLLO

I come to testify. This man, by observed law,
came to me as suppliant, took his place by my hearth and hall,
and it was I who cleaned him of the stain of blood.
I have also come to help him win his case. I bear
responsibility for his mother's murder.

(To Athena.)

You   580
who know the rules, initiate the trial. Preside.

ATHENA   *(To the Furies.)*
I declare the trial opened. Yours is the first word.
For it must justly be the accuser who speaks first
and opens the case, and makes plain what the action is.

CHORUS LEADER
We are many, but we shall cut it short. You, then,   585
word against word answer our charges one by one.
Say first, did you kill your mother or did you not?

ORESTES
Yes, I killed her. There shall be no denial of that.

CHORUS LEADER
There are three falls in the match and one has gone to us.

ORESTES
So you say. But you have not even thrown your man.   590

CHORUS LEADER
So. Then how did you kill her? You are bound to say.

ORESTES
I do. With drawn sword in my hand I cut her throat.

CHORUS LEADER
By whose persuasion and advice did you do this?

ORESTES
By order of this god, here. So he testifies.

CHORUS LEADER
The prophet god guided you into this matricide?   595

ORESTES
Yes. I have never complained of this. I do not now.

[27] THE EUMENIDES

CHORUS LEADER

When sentence seizes you, you will talk a different way.

ORESTES

I have no fear. My father will aid me from the grave.

CHORUS LEADER

Kill your mother, then put trust in a corpse! Trust on.

ORESTES

Yes. She was polluted twice over with disgrace.   600

CHORUS LEADER

Tell me how, and explain it to the judges here.

ORESTES

She murdered her husband, and thereby my father too.

CHORUS LEADER

Of this stain, death has set her free. But you still live.

ORESTES

While she lived, why did you not descend and drive her out?

CHORUS LEADER

The man she killed was not of blood congenital.   605

ORESTES

But do I then share with my mother a blood bond?

CHORUS LEADER

Yes, you butcher. How else could she have nursed you in
her womb? Do you forswear your mother's intimate blood?

ORESTES

Yours to bear witness now, Apollo, and expound
the case for me, if I was right to cut her down.   610
I will not deny I did this thing, because I did
do it. But was the bloodshed right or not? Decide
and answer. As you answer, I shall state my case.

APOLLO

To you, judges, established by Athena in your power,
I shall speak justly. I am a prophet, I shall not 615
lie. Never, for man, woman, nor city, from my throne
of prophecy have I spoken a word, except
that which Zeus, father of Olympians, might command.
This is justice. Recognize then how great its strength.
I tell you, follow our father's will. For not even 620
the oath that binds you is more strong than Zeus is strong.

CHORUS LEADER

Then Zeus, as you say, authorized the oracle
to this Orestes, stating he could wreak the death
of his father on his mother, and it would have no force?

APOLLO

It is not the same thing for a noble man to die, 625
one honored with the king's staff given by the hand of god,
and that by means of a woman, not with the far cast
of fierce arrows, as an Amazon might have done,
but in a way that you shall hear, O Pallas and you
who sit in state to judge this action by your vote. 630

He had come home from his campaigning. He had done
better than worse, in the eyes of a fair judge. She lay
in wait for him. It was the bath.° When he was at
its edge, she hooded the robe on him, and in the blind
and complex toils tangled her man, and chopped him down. 635

That is the story of the death of a great man,
revered in all men's sight, lord of the host of ships.
I have called the woman what she was, so that the people
whose duty it is to try this case may be inflamed.

CHORUS LEADER

Zeus, by your story, gives first place to the father's death. 640
Yet Zeus himself shackled elder Cronus, his own

father. Is this not contradiction? I testify,
judges, that this is being said in your hearing.

APOLLO

You foul animals, from whom the gods turn in disgust,
Zeus could undo shackles, such hurt can be made good,   645
and there is every kind of way to get out. But once
the dust has drained down all a man's blood, once the man
has died, there is no raising of him up again.
This is a thing for which my father never made
curative spells. All other states, without effort   650
of hard breath, he can completely rearrange.

CHORUS LEADER

See what it means to force acquittal of this man.
He has spilled his mother's blood upon the ground. Shall he
then be at home in Argos in his father's house?
What altars of the community shall he use? Is there   655
a brotherhood's lustration that will let him in?

APOLLO

I will tell you, and I will answer correctly. Watch.
The mother is no parent of that which is called
her child, but only nurse of the new-planted seed
that grows. The parent is he who mounts. A stranger she   660
preserves a stranger's seed, if no god interfere.
I will show you proof of what I have explained. There can
be a father without any mother. There she stands,
the living witness, daughter of Olympian Zeus,
she who was never fostered in the dark of the womb   665
yet such a child as no goddess could bring to birth.
In all else, Pallas, as I best may understand,
I shall make great your city and its populace.
So I have brought this man to sit beside the hearth
of your house, to be your true friend for the rest of time,   670
so you shall win him, goddess, to fight by your side,
and among men to come this shall stand a strong bond
that his and your own people's children shall be friends.

ATHENA

Shall I assume that enough has now been said, and tell
the judges to render what they believe a true verdict?   675

CHORUS LEADER

Every arrow we had has been shot now. We wait
on their decision, to see how the case has gone.

ATHENA

So then. How shall I act correctly in your eyes?

APOLLO

You have heard what you have heard, and as you cast your
    votes,
good friends, respect in your hearts the oath that you have
    sworn.   680

ATHENA

If it please you, men of Attica, hear my decree
now, as you judge this case, the first trial for bloodshed.
For Aegeus' population, this forevermore
shall be the ground where justices deliberate.
Here is the Hill of Ares, here the Amazons   685
encamped and built their shelters when they came in arms
in rage at Theseus, here they piled their rival towers
to rise, a new city against his city long ago,
and sacrificed for Ares. So this rock is named
from then the Hill of Ares. Here the reverence   690
of citizens, their fear and kindred do-no-wrong
shall hold by day and in the blessing of night alike
all while the people do not muddy their own laws
with foul infusions. But if bright water you stain
with mud, you nevermore will find it fit to drink.   695
No anarchy, no rule of a single master. Thus
I advise my citizens to govern and to grace,
and not to cast fear utterly from your city. What
man who fears nothing at all is ever righteous? Such
be your just terrors, and you may deserve and have   700

salvation for your citadel, your land's defense,
such as is nowhere else found among men, neither
among the Scythians, nor the land that Pelops held.
I establish this tribunal. It shall be untouched
by money making, grave but quick to wrath, watchful   705
to protect those who sleep, a sentry on the land.
These words I have spun out are for my citizens,
advice into the future. All must stand upright
now, take each man his ballot in his hand, think on
his oath, and make his judgment. For my word is said.   710

(One by one, the eleven mortal jurors walk forward to place their
voting pebble into an urn: each time, Apollo or the Chorus speaks.)

CHORUS LEADER
I give you counsel by no means to disregard
this company. We can be a weight to crush your land.

APOLLO
I speak too. I command you to fear, and not
make void the yield of oracles from Zeus and me.

CHORUS LEADER
You honor bloody actions where you have no right.   715
The oracles you give shall be no longer clean.

APOLLO
My father's purposes are twisted then. For he
was appealed to by Ixion, the first murderer.

CHORUS LEADER
Talk! But for my part, if I do not win the case,
I shall come back to this land and it will feel my weight.   720

APOLLO
Neither among the elder nor the younger gods
have you consideration. I shall win this suit.

CHORUS LEADER

Such was your action in the house of Pheres. Then
you beguiled the Fates to let mortals go free from death.

APOLLO

Is it not right to help the man who shows respect   725
and piety, above all when he stands in need?

CHORUS LEADER

You won the ancient goddesses over with wine
and so destroyed the orders of an elder time.

APOLLO

You shall not win the issue of this suit, but shall
be made to void your poison to no enemy's hurt.   730

CHORUS LEADER

Since you, a young god, would ride down my elder age,
I must stay here and listen to how the trial goes,
being yet uncertain to loose my anger on the state.

ATHENA

It is my task to render final judgment here.
This is a ballot for Orestes I shall cast.   735
There is no mother anywhere who gave me birth,
and, but for marriage, I am always for the male
with all my heart, and strongly on my father's side.
So, in a case where the wife has killed her husband, lord
of the house, I shall not value her death more highly than his.   740
And even if the votes are equal, Orestes is the winner.
You of the jurymen who have this duty assigned,
shake out the ballots from the vessels, with all speed.

ORESTES

Phoebus Apollo, what will the decision be?

CHORUS LEADER

Darkness of night, our mother, are you here to watch?   745

ORESTES

This is the end for me. The noose, or else the light.

CHORUS LEADER

Here our destruction, or our high duties confirmed.

APOLLO

Shake out the votes accurately, Athenian friends.
Be careful as you pick them up. Make no mistake.
In the lapse of judgment great disaster comes. The cast   750
of a single ballot can restore a house entire.

ATHENA

The man before us has escaped the charge of blood.
The ballots are in equal number for each side.

ORESTES

Pallas Athena, you have kept my house alive.
When I had lost the land of my fathers you gave me   755
a place to live. Among the Hellenes they shall say:
"A man of Argos lives again in the estates
of his father, all by grace of Pallas Athena, and
Apollo, and with them the all-ordaining god
the Savior"—who remembers my father's death, who looked   760
upon my mother's advocates, and rescues me.
I shall go home now, but before I go I swear
to this your country and to this your multitude
of people into all the bigness of time to be,
that never man who holds the helm of my state shall come   765
against your country in the ordered strength of spears,
but though I lie then in my grave, I still shall wreak
helpless bad luck and misadventure upon all
who step across the oath that I have sworn: their ways
disconsolate make, their crossings full of evil   770
augury, so they shall be sorry that they moved.
But while they keep the upright way, and hold in high
regard the city of Pallas, and align their spears
to fight beside her, I shall be their gracious spirit.

And so farewell, you and your city's populace.   775
May you outwrestle and overthrow all those who come
against you, to your safety and your spears' success.°

(Exit Orestes to the side. Exit also Apollo.)

CHORUS [*singing throughout this interchange with Athena, who speaks
in response*]
  Gods of the younger generation, you have ridden down
  the laws of the elder time, torn them out of my hands.
  I, disinherited, suffering, heavy with anger   780
  shall let loose on the land
  the vindictive poison
  dripping deadly out of my heart upon the ground;
  this from itself shall breed
  cancer, the leafless, the barren   785
  to strike, for the right, their low lands
  and drag its smear of mortal infection on the ground.
  What shall I do? Afflicted
  I am mocked by these people.
  I have borne what cannot   790
  be borne. Great the sorrows and the dishonor upon
  the sad daughters of Night.

ATHENA
  Listen to me. I would not have you be so grieved.
  For you have not been beaten. This was the result   795
  of a fair ballot which ended up even. You were not
  dishonored, but the luminous evidence of Zeus
  was there, and he who spoke the oracle was he
  who ordered Orestes so to act and not be hurt.
  Do not be angry any longer with this land   800
  nor bring the bulk of your hatred down on it; do not
  render it barren of fruit, nor spill the dripping rain
  of death in fierce and jagged lines to eat the seeds.
  In complete honesty I promise you a place
  of your own, deep hidden underground that is yours by right   805

where you shall sit on shining chairs beside the hearth
to accept devotions offered by your citizens.

CHORUS

Gods of the younger generation, you have ridden down
the laws of the elder time, torn them out of my hands.
I, disinherited, suffering, heavy with anger   810
shall let loose on the land
the vindictive poison
dripping deadly out of my heart upon the ground;
this from itself shall breed
cancer, the leafless, the barren   815
to strike, for the right, their low lands
and drag its smear of mortal infection on the ground.
What shall I do? Afflicted
I am mocked by these people.
I have borne what cannot   820
be borne. Great the sorrow and the dishonor upon
the sad daughters of Night.

ATHENA

No, not dishonored. You are goddesses. Do not
in too much anger make this place of mortal men   825
uninhabitable. I have Zeus behind me. Do
we need to speak of that? I am the only god
who knows the keys to where his thunderbolts are locked.
We do not need such, do we? Be reasonable
and do not from a reckless mouth cast on the land   830
spells that will ruin every thing which might bear fruit.
No. Put to sleep the bitter strength in the black wave
and live with me and share my pride of worship. Here
is a big land, and from it you shall win first fruits
in offerings for children and the marriage rite   835
for always. Then you will say my argument was good.

CHORUS

That they could treat me so!

I, the mind of the past, to be driven under the ground
outcast, like dirt!
The wind I breathe is fury and utter hate.   840
Earth, ah, Earth
what is this agony that crawls under my ribs?
Night, hear me, O Night,
mother. They have wiped me out   845
and the hard hands of the gods
and their treacheries have taken my old rights away.

ATHENA

I will bear your angers. You are elder born than I
and in that you are wiser far than I. Yet still
Zeus gave me too intelligence not to be despised.   850
If you go away into some land of foreigners,
I warn you, you will come to yearn for this country.
Time in forward flood shall ever grow more dignified
for the people of this city. And you, in your place
of eminence beside Erechtheus in his house   855
shall win from female and from male processionals
more than all lands of men beside could ever give.
Only in this place that I haunt do not inflict
your bloody stimulus to twist the inward hearts
of young men, raging in a fury not of wine,   860
nor, as if taking the heart from fighting cocks,
engraft among my citizens that spirit of war
that turns their battle fury inward on themselves.
No, let our wars range outward—may they range full fierce
and terrible, for those desiring high renown.   865
No true fighter I call the bird that fights at home.
Such life I offer you, and it is yours to take.
Do good, receive good, and be honored as the good
are honored. Share our country, the beloved of god.

CHORUS

That they could treat me so!   870
I, the mind of the past, to be driven under the ground

outcast, like dirt!
The wind I breathe is fury and utter hate.
Earth, ah, Earth
what is this agony that crawls under my ribs?   875
Night, hear me, O Night,
mother. They have wiped me out
and the hard hands of the gods
and their treacheries have taken my old rights away.   880

ATHENA
I will not weary of telling you all the good things
I offer, so that you can never say that you,
an elder god, were driven unfriended from the land
by me in my youth, and by my mortal citizens.
But if you hold Persuasion has her sacred place   885
of worship, in the sweet beguilement of my voice,
then you might stay with us. But if you wish to stay
then it would not be justice to inflict your rage
upon this city, your resentment or bad luck
to armies. You can be landholders in this country   890
if you will, in all justice, with full privilege.

CHORUS LEADER [*speaking*]
Lady Athena, what is this place you say is mine?

ATHENA
A place free of all grief and pain. Take it for yours.

CHORUS LEADER
If I do take it, shall I have some definite powers?

ATHENA
No household shall be prosperous without your will.   895

CHORUS LEADER
You will do this? You will really let me be so strong?

ATHENA
So we shall straighten the lives of all who worship us.

CHORUS LEADER
You guarantee such honor for the rest of time?

ATHENA
I have no need to promise what I cannot do.

CHORUS LEADER
I think you will have your way with me. My hate is going.   900

ATHENA
Stay here, then, in this land, and gain others too as friends.

CHORUS LEADER
I will put a spell upon the land. What shall it be?

ATHENA
Something that has no traffic with evil success.
Let it come out of the ground, out of the sea's water,
and from the high air make the waft of gentle gales   905
wash over the country in full sunlight, and the seed
and stream of the soil's yield and of the grazing beasts
be strong and never fail our people as time goes,
and make the human seed be kept alive. Make more
the issue of those who worship more your ways, for as   910
the gardener works in love, so love I best of all
the unblighted generation of these upright men.
All such is yours for granting. In the speech and show
and pride of battle, I myself shall not endure
this city's eclipse in the estimation of mankind.   915

CHORUS [singing throughout the following interchange with Athena,
who chants in response]
                    STROPHE A
I accept this home at Athena's side.
I shall not forget the cause
of this city, which Zeus all powerful and Ares
rule, stronghold of divinities,
glory of Hellene gods, their guarded altar.   920
So with forecast of good

I sing this prayer for them
that the sun's bright magnificence shall break out wave
on wave of all the happiness 925
life can give, across their land.

ATHENA

Here are my actions. In all goodwill
toward these citizens I establish in power
these great divinities, difficult to soften.
To them is given the handling entire 930
of men's lives. That man
who has felt the full weight of their hands°
takes the strokes of life, knows not whence, not why,
for crimes wreaked in past generations
drag him before these powers. Loud his voice 935
but the silent doom
hates hard, and breaks him to dust.

CHORUS

ANTISTROPHE A

Let there blow no wind that wrecks the trees.
I pronounce words of grace.
Nor blaze of heat blind the blossoms of grown plants, nor 940
cross the circles of its right
place. Let no barren deadly sickness creep and kill.
May flocks fatten. Earth be kind
to them, with double fold of fruit 945
in time appointed for its yielding. Secret child
of Earth, her hidden wealth, bestow
blessing and surprise of gods.

ATHENA

Strong guard of our city, hear you these
and what they portend? Fury is a high queen 950
of strength even among the immortal gods
and the undergods, and for humankind
they accomplish their work, absolute, clear:

for some, singing; for some, life dimmed
in tears; theirs the disposition.   955

CHORUS

Death of manhood cut down
before its prime I forbid:
girls' grace and glory find
men to live life with them.
Grant, you who have the power.   960
And O, steering spirits of law,
goddesses of Destiny,
sisters from my mother, hear;
in all houses implicated,
in all time heavy of hand   965
on whom your just arrest falls,
most august among goddesses.

ATHENA
It is my glory to hear how these
generosities
are given my land. I admire the eyes   970
of Persuasion, who guided the speech of my mouth
toward these, when they were reluctant and wild.
Zeus, who guides men's speech in councils, was too
strong; and my ambition
for good wins out in the whole issue.   975

CHORUS

This my prayer: civil war
fattening on men's ruin shall
not thunder in our city. Let
not the dry dust that drinks
the black blood of citizens   980
through passion for revenge
and bloodshed for bloodshed

be given our state to prey upon.
Let them render grace for grace.
Let love be their common will; 985
let them hate with single heart.
Much wrong in the world thereby is healed.

ATHENA

Are they taking thought to discover that road
where speech goes straight?
In the fearsome look of the faces of these 990
I see great good for our citizens.
While with goodwill you hold in high honor
these Kindly Spirits, their will shall be good, as you steer
your city, your land
on an upright course clear through to the end. 995

CHORUS

STROPHE C

Farewell, farewell. High destiny shall be yours
by right. Farewell, citizens
seated near the throne of Zeus,
beloved by the Maiden he loves,
civilized as years go by, 1000
sheltered under Athena's wings,
revered in her father's sight.

ATHENA

Goddesses, farewell. Mine to lead, as these
attend us, to where
by the sacred light new chambers are given. 1005
Go then. Sped by majestic sacrifice
from these, plunge beneath the ground. There hold
off what might hurt the land; pour in
the city's advantage, success in the end.
You, children of Cranaus, you who keep 1010
the citadel, guide these guests of the state.

For good things given,
your hearts' desire be for good to return.

CHORUS

Farewell and again farewell, words spoken twice over,
all who by this citadel,   1015
mortal men, spirits divine,
hold the city of Pallas, grace
this my guestship in your land.
Life will give you no regrets.   1020

(A second Chorus, of women of Attica, begins to enter, from the side.)

ATHENA [*now speaking*]
    Well said. I assent to all the burden of your prayers,
    and by the light of flaring torches now attend
    your passage to the deep and subterranean hold,
    as by us walk those women whose high privilege
    it is to guard my image. Flower of all the land   1025
    of Theseus, let them issue now, grave companies,
    maidens, wives, elder women, in processional.°
    In the investiture of purple-stained robes
    dignify them, and let the torchlight go before
    so that the kindly company of these within   1030
    our ground may shine in the future of strong men to come.

(The first Chorus begin to replace their black
robes with reddish-purple ones.)

SECOND CHORUS [*singing*]

STROPHE A

Home, home, O high, O aspiring
Daughters of Night, aged children, in kindly processional.
Bless them, all here, with words of good omen.   1035

ANTISTROPHE A

In the primeval dark of earth-hollows

held in high veneration with rights sacrificial
bless them, all people, with words of good omen.

Wish favor, wish justice for this land,   1040
and follow, august goddesses, flushed in the flamesprung
torchlight, delighting in your journey.
Singing all follow our footsteps.

There shall be peace forever between these people
of Pallas and their guests. Zeus the all-seeing   1045
joined with Destiny to confirm it.
Singing all follow our footsteps.

(Everybody departs, in procession.)

PHILOCTETES

SOPHOCLES
Translated by David Grene

INTRODUCTION TO SOPHOCLES' PHILOCTETES

Philoctetes was produced in 409 BCE, when Sophocles was over eighty years old, and won first prize.

Philoctetes was the hero who inherited the great bow of Heracles. He joined the Achaean expedition against Troy, but in guiding his comrades to a place of sacrifice he was bitten in the foot by a snake, and the wound would not heal. Because of the stench of the festering sore and the man's inauspicious cries, he was marooned on the (in this version uninhabited) island of Lemnos. But after the death of Achilles, the Greeks found from prophecies that they could not take Troy without Philoctetes and his bow, and therefore had to send an embassy to beg or beguile or force him to come back. Restored and healed at last, he was to play a leading part in the final battles at Troy. (The story is told in the epic continuations of Homer, barely noticed, though obviously known, by Homer himself.) Many ancient Greek plays called *Philoctetes* are recorded, but all except the one by Sophocles are lost. Aeschylus produced one, of unknown date, and so did Euripides, along with *Medea* in 431 BCE.

The circumstances of the wound and the plight of Philoctetes, the identity of the hero or heroes assigned to reclaim him, the means used—these vary in the tradition. Here, to Odysseus, the intelligent, persistent, ruthless spirit of the Greek war against Troy, Sophocles has added as collaborator the young Neoptolemus, son of Achilles and pre-eminent fighting man, who, schooled by Odysseus, succeeds in winning the bow from Philoctetes. But he acts against his nature in so doing. Caught between military duty and his own personal integrity, he must, as a Sophoclean hero, follow the dictates of the latter. At the end, he is ready to give up his career of glory and the cause of the Trojan War. Only the command of the deified Heracles saves the situation and brings about the necessary outcome for all three of the main characters.

PHILOCTETES

Characters   ODYSSEUS
                NEOPTOLEMUS, son of Achilles
                CHORUS of Neoptolemus' sailors
                PHILOCTETES
                A SAILOR, disguised as a Merchant
                HERACLES

Scene: A lonely spot on the island of Lemnos, with the two entrances to a cave.

          (Enter Odysseus and Neoptolemus with a sailor from the side.)

ODYSSEUS
    This is it; this is Lemnos and its beach
    down to the surrounding sea; desolate, untrodden
    by humans. Here I marooned him long ago,
    the son of Poias, the Malian, his foot   5
    diseased and eaten away with running ulcers.
        Son of our greatest hero,
    son of Achilles, Neoptolemus,
    I did what I was ordered by the kings, our commanders.
    We had no peace with him: at the holy festivals,
    we dared not touch the wine and meat; he screamed
    and groaned so, and those terrible cries of his
    brought ill luck on our celebrations; all
    the camp was haunted by him.   10
    Now is no time to talk to you of this,
    now is no time for long speeches.

I am afraid that he may hear of my coming
and ruin all my plans to take him.
It is you who must help me with the rest. Look about   15
and see where there might be a cave with two mouths.
There are two niches to rest in, one in the sun
when it is cold, the other a tunneled passage
through which the breezes blow sleep in summertime.
To the left, a little, you may see a spring—   20
if it is still unchoked—go this way quietly,
see if he's there or somewhere else and signal.
Then I can tell you the rest. Listen:
I shall tell you. We will both do this thing.   25

NEOPTOLEMUS
What you speak of is near at hand, Odysseus.
I think I see such a cave.

ODYSSEUS
Above or below? I cannot see it myself.

NEOPTOLEMUS
Above here, and no sound of any feet.

ODYSSEUS
Look, in case he is housed within, asleep.   30

NEOPTOLEMUS
I see an empty dwelling, with no one there.

ODYSSEUS
And nothing to keep house with?

NEOPTOLEMUS
A pallet bed, stuffed with leaves, for someone's sleep.

ODYSSEUS
And nothing else? Nothing inside the house?

NEOPTOLEMUS
A cup, made of a single block, a poor   35
workman's contrivance. And some kindling, too.

ODYSSEUS

It is his treasure house that you describe.

NEOPTOLEMUS

And look, some rags are drying in the sun
full of the oozing matter from a sore.

ODYSSEUS

Yes, certainly he lives here, even now   40
he's somewhere not far off. He cannot go far,
sick as he is, lame cripple for so long.
It's likely he has gone to search for food
or somewhere that he knows there is an herb
to ease his pain. Send your man here to watch,   45
that he may not come upon me without warning.
For he would rather take me than all the other Greeks.

NEOPTOLEMUS

Very well, then, the path will be watched.

(Exit Sailor to the side.)

Go on with your story; tell me what you want.

ODYSSEUS

Son of Achilles,   50
our coming here has a purpose; to it be loyal
with more than just your body. If you should hear
some strange new thing, unlike what you have heard
before, still serve us; it was to serve you came here.

NEOPTOLEMUS

What would you have me do?

ODYSSEUS

                         Ensnare
the soul of Philoctetes with your words.   55
When he asks who you are and whence you came,
say you are Achilles' son; you need not lie.
Say you are sailing home, leaving the Greeks

and all their fleet, in bitter hatred. Say
that they had prayed you, urged you from your home,   60
and swore that only with your help
could Troy be taken. Yet when you came and asked,
as by your right, to have your father's arms,
Achilles' arms, they did not think you worthy
but gave them to Odysseus. Say what you will
against me; do not spare me anything.   65
Nothing of this will hurt me; if you will not
do this, you will bring sorrow on all the Greeks.
If this man's bow shall not be taken by us,
you cannot ever sack the land of Troy.

Perhaps you wonder why you can safely meet him,   70
why he would trust you and not me. Let me explain.
You have come here unforced, unpledged by oaths,
made no part of our earlier expedition.
The opposite is true in my own case;
at no point can I deny his charge.
If, when he sees me, Philoctetes   75
still has his bow, there is an end of me;
and you too, for your presence with me, would die.
For this you must sharpen your wits, to become a thief
of the arms no man has conquered.

I know, young man, it is not your natural bent
to say such things nor to contrive such mischief.   80
But the prize of victory is pleasant to win.
Bear up: another time we shall prove honest.
For one brief shameless portion of a day
give me yourself, and then for all the rest
you may be called most scrupulous of men.   85

NEOPTOLEMUS
Son of Laertes, what I dislike to hear
I hate to put in execution.
I have a natural antipathy
to get my ends by tricks and stratagems.

So, too, they say, my father was. I am quite ready
to fight and capture this man, bring him by force,   90
but not by treachery. Surely a one-legged man
cannot prevail against so many of us!
I recognize that I was sent with you
to follow your instructions. I am loath
to have you call me traitor. Still, my lord,
I would prefer even to fail with honor   95
than win by cheating.

ODYSSEUS
You are a good man's son.
I was young, too, once, and then I had a tongue
very inactive and a doing hand.
Now when I go out to face the test, I see
that everywhere among the race of mortals
it is the tongue that wins and not the deed.

NEOPTOLEMUS
What do you tell me to do, except tell lies?   100

ODYSSEUS
I'm telling you to use a trick to take Philoctetes.

NEOPTOLEMUS
And why must I use a trick, rather than persuasion?

ODYSSEUS
He will not be persuaded, and force will fail.

NEOPTOLEMUS
Has he such strength to give him confidence?

ODYSSEUS
The arrows none may avoid that carry death.   105

NEOPTOLEMUS
Then even to encounter him is not safe?

ODYSSEUS
Not if you do not take him by a trick, as I say.

NEOPTOLEMUS

Do you not find it shameful to tell lies?

ODYSSEUS

Not if the lying brings our rescue with it.

NEOPTOLEMUS

How can a man not blush to say such things?   110

ODYSSEUS

When one does something for gain, one need not blush.

NEOPTOLEMUS

What gain for me that he should come to Troy?

ODYSSEUS

Only his weapons are destined to take Troy.

NEOPTOLEMUS

Then *I* shall not be, as was said, its conqueror?

ODYSSEUS

Not you without them, nor they without you.   115

NEOPTOLEMUS

They must be my quarry then, if this is so.

ODYSSEUS

You will win a double prize if you do this.

NEOPTOLEMUS

What? If I know, I will do what you say.

ODYSSEUS

You'd be called both a wise man and a good one.

NEOPTOLEMUS

Well, then I will do it, casting aside all shame.   120

ODYSSEUS

You clearly recollect all I have told you?

NEOPTOLEMUS

Yes, now that I have consented to it.

ODYSSEUS

                    Stay
and wait his coming here; I will go
so he may not spy my presence.
I will dispatch the scout back to the ship;   125
and if you are too slow, I will send him back here again,
disguised as a sea captain; so Philoctetes
will never know him.
Whatever clever story he presents, then   130
go along with it and use it as you need.
Now I will go to the ship and leave you in charge.
May Hermes, god of tricks, the escort, for us
be guide indeed, and Victory and Athena,
city protector, who preserves me always.

          (*Exit Odysseus to the side. The Chorus enters from the other side.*)

CHORUS [*singing*]

                    STROPHE A
We are strangers, my lord, and this land is strange;   135
what shall we say and what conceal from this suspicious man?
Tell us.
For one man's artful skill outdoes another's,
and his judgment too, if there resides
in his sovereign keeping Zeus's holy scepter.   140
To you, young lord, all this has come,
all the power of your forefathers. So tell us now
what we must do to serve you.

NEOPTOLEMUS [*chanting*]
Now—if you wish to see where he rests   145
on his crag at the edge—look, be not afraid.
But when the terrible wanderer returns,
the one who lives in this place, then watch
my signals and take your cues from me.
Help when you can.

CHORUS [*singing*]

ANTISTROPHE A

This we have always done, my lord,   150
have kept a watchful eye over your safety.
But now
tell us what places he inhabits
and where he stays. It is important   155
for us to know this,
lest he attack us unawares.
Where does he live? Where does he rest?
What footpath does he follow? Is he at home or away?

NEOPTOLEMUS [*chanting*]

This, that you see, is his two-doored home,
where he sleeps on the rock.   160

CHORUS [*chanting*]

Where is he gone, unhappy creature?

NEOPTOLEMUS [*chanting*]

I am sure
he has gone to find food somewhere near here;
stumbling, lame, dragging along the path,
he is trying to shoot birds to prolong his miserable life.
This indeed, they say, is how he lives.   165
And no one comes near to cure him.

CHORUS [*singing*]

STROPHE B

Yes, for my part I pity him:
how unhappy, how utterly alone, always   170
he suffers the savagery of his illness
alone, with no one to care for him,
with no friendly face near him,
but bewildered and distraught at each need as it comes.   175
How does the poor man hold out?
Oh powers divine,° oh unhappy generations of mortals
whose lives suffer extremes!

This man is as well born perhaps as any,   180
second to no son of an ancient house.
Yet now his life lacks everything,
and he makes his bed all alone,
with spotted and shaggy beasts for neighbors—
piteous in his pain and hunger,   185
suffering with incurable wretchedness;
there is only a blabbering echo,
that comes from the distance in response
to his bitter crying.   190

NEOPTOLEMUS [*chanting*]

I am not surprised at any of this:
this is a god's doing, if I have any understanding.
These afflictions that have come upon him
are the work of Chryse, bitter of heart.
As for his present loneliness and suffering,   195
this, too, no doubt is part of some god's plan
that he may not bend against Troy
the divine invincible bow
until the time has come, at which, so it's said,
Troy must indeed be conquered by it.   200

CHORUS

Hush.

NEOPTOLEMUS

What is it?

CHORUS [*singing*]

STROPHE C

Hush! I hear a sound,
the sound of a man in pain.
Is it here? Is it there?°
I hear a voice, now I can hear it clearly,   205
the voice of a man, moving along the path,
hard put to it to walk. It's far away,

but I can hear it; I can hear the sound well,
the voice of a man wounded; it is quite clear now.
Come now, my son.   210

NEOPTOLEMUS
Tell me, what?

CHORUS

ANTISTROPHE C
Time for new plans. He is here, almost with us.
His is no cheerful marching to the pipe
like a shepherd with his flock.
No, a bitter cry.
He must have stumbled far down on the path,   215
and his moaning carried all the way here.
Or perhaps he saw the ship in the unfriendly harbor,°
for it was a bitter cry.

(Enter Philoctetes, from the side.)

PHILOCTETES
Strangers, who are you that have put in, rowing   220
to a shore without houses or anchorage?
What countrymen may I call you? Who are your people?
Greeks you seem in clothing—dear to me.
May I hear your voice? Do not be afraid   225
or shrink from such as I am, grown a savage.
I have been alone and very wretched,
without friend or comrade, suffering a great deal.
Take pity on me; speak to me, if indeed
you come as friends.
Please—answer me.   230
It is not right for me not to get this from you,
or you from me.

NEOPTOLEMUS
Stranger, for your questions, since you wish to know,
know we are Greeks.

PHILOCTETES
>Friendliest of tongues!
That I should hear it spoken once again   235
by such a man after long years! My boy,
who are you? Why have you come here? What has brought
>you?
What impulse? What friendliest of winds?
Tell me all this, that I may know who you are.

NEOPTOLEMUS
By birth, I'm from Scyrus that the sea surrounds;
I am sailing home. My name is Neoptolemus,   240
Achilles' son. Now you know everything.

PHILOCTETES
Son of a father that I loved so dearly
and of a land I loved, you that were reared
by that old man Lycomedes, what kind of venture
can have brought you to port here? Where did you sail from?

NEOPTOLEMUS
At present I am bound from Troy.   245

PHILOCTETES
>From Troy?
But you did not sail with us to Troy at first.

NEOPTOLEMUS
You, then, are one that also had a share
in all that trouble?

PHILOCTETES
>Is it possible
you do not know me, boy, me whom you see here?

NEOPTOLEMUS
I never saw you before. How could I know you?   250

PHILOCTETES
You never heard my name then? Never a rumor
of all my terrible sufferings, even to death?

NEOPTOLEMUS

I never knew a word of what you ask me.

PHILOCTETES

Surely I must be wretched, and hated by gods   255
that never a word of me, of how I live here,
should have reached home or anywhere in Greece.
Yet those who cast me away so impiously
keep quiet about it and laugh, while my disease
always increases and grows worse. My boy,
you are Achilles' son. I that stand here   260
am one you may have heard of, as the master
of Heracles' arms. I am Philoctetes
the son of Poias. Those two generals
and Odysseus king of the Cephallenians   265
cast me ashore here to their shame, alone,
wasting with my sickness caused by the murderous bite
of a viper mortally dangerous.
Alone with this disease they left me here
when our fleet put in on its way from the isle of Chryse.   270
They were happy when they saw that I had fallen asleep
on the shore in a rocky cave, after a rough passage.
They went away and left me with some rags—
as if for a beggar—and a handful of food.   275
May the gods give them the like!
Think, boy, of that awakening when I awoke
and found them gone; think of the useless tears
and groans for my condition, when I saw the ships—
which I had once commanded—gone, and not
a single man left there on the island,   280
no one to help me or to lend a hand
when I was seized with my sickness. I looked around:
in all I saw before me nothing but pain;
but of that a great abundance, boy.

Time came and went for me. In my tiny shelter   285
I must alone do everything for myself.

To meet my belly's needs, this bow of mine
shot pigeons as they flew by; then I must drag
my cursed foot, to where the feathered bolt
sped by the bow's thong had struck down a bird.   290
If I must drink, and it was wintertime—
the water was frozen—I must break up firewood.
Again I crawled and miserably contrived
to do the work. Whenever I had no fire,   295
rubbing stone on stone I would at last produce
the spark that kept me still in life.
A roof for shelter, provided I have fire,
gives me everything but release from pain.

Boy, let me tell you of this island.   300
No sailor by his choice comes near it.
There is no anchorage, nor anywhere
that one can land, sell goods, be entertained.
Sensible men make no voyages here.
Yet now and then someone arrives—not on purpose,   305
but time as long as this allows much to happen.
When they have come here, boy, they pity me—
at least they say they do—and in their pity
they have given me scraps of food and cast-off clothes;
but that other thing, when I dare mention it,   310
none of them will—to bring me home again.

It is nine years now that I have spent dying,
with hunger and pain feeding my insatiable
disease. That, boy, is what they have done to me,
the two Atridae, and mighty Odysseus.
May the gods that live on Olympus grant   315
that they pay for this, agony for my agony.

CHORUS LEADER
   In this, I too resemble your other visitors.
   I pity you, son of Poias.

NEOPTOLEMUS

       I am a witness,
I also, of the truth of what you say.
I know it is true. I have dealt with those villains,
the two Atridae and the lord Odysseus.

PHILOCTETES

Have you, as well as I, then suffered wrong
from the cursed Atridae, so as to be angry at them?

NEOPTOLEMUS

Give me the chance to gratify my anger
with my hand some day!
Then will Mycenae and Sparta come to know
that Scyrus too is mother to valiant men.

PHILOCTETES

       Well said, boy!
You come to me with a great hate against them.
Because of what?

NEOPTOLEMUS

       I will tell you, Philoctetes—
for all that it hurts to tell it—
of how I came to Troy and what dishonor
they put upon me.
       When fatefully Achilles came to die ...

PHILOCTETES

O stop! tell me no more. Let me understand
this first. Is he dead, the son of Peleus, dead?

NEOPTOLEMUS

Yes, he is dead; no man his conqueror
but shot by a god, they say, Phoebus the archer.

PHILOCTETES

Noble was he that killed and he that died.
Boy, I am at a loss which to do first,
ask for your story or to mourn for him.

NEOPTOLEMUS

I would think that your own sufferings were quite enough,
poor man, without mourning for those of others.   340

PHILOCTETES

Yes, that is true. So again, tell me your story
of how they have insulted you.

NEOPTOLEMUS
                              They came
for me, did great Odysseus and the man
that was my father's tutor, with a ship
wonderfully decked with ribbons. They had a story—
be it truth or lie—that it was divine decree   345
that no one else, since he, my father, was dead,
but I and I alone should take the towers of Troy.
        This was their story. And sir, it didn't take long
for me quickly to embark with them.
Chiefly, you know, I was prompted by my yearning   350
for the dead man. I had hope of seeing him
while still unburied. Alive I never had.
And in addition, it was a splendid notion
that I could go and capture the city of Troy.
We had a favoring wind; on the second day   355
we touched Sigeum. As I disembarked,
all of the soldiers swarmed around me, blessed me,
swore that they saw Achilles alive again,
now gone from them forever. But he still lay
unburied. I, his ill-fated son, wept for him;   360
then, in a while, I came to the two Atridae,
my friends,° as it seemed right to do, and asked them
for my father's weapons and the other things of his.
They needed brazen faces for their answer:
"Son of Achilles, all that your father had,   365
all else, is yours to take, but not his weapons.
Another man now owns them, Laertes' son."
I burst into tears, jumped up, enraged,

cried out in my pain, "You scoundrels, did you dare
to give those arms that were mine to someone else 370
before I knew of it?" Then Odysseus
spoke—he was standing near me—"Yes, and rightly,"
he said, "they gave them, boy. For it was I
who rescued them and him, their former owner."
My anger got the better of me; I cursed him outright
with every insult that I knew, sparing nothing, 375
if he should take my arms away from me.
And he, a man not usually given to quarreling,
was stung by what I said. He answered me:
"You were not where we were. You were at home,
out of the reach of duty. And since, besides,
you have so bold a tongue in your head, never 380
will you possess these arms to bring back home to Scyrus."
There it was. Abused, insulted, I lost
what should be mine and so sailed home. Odysseus,
that filthy son of filthy parents, robbed me.
Yet I do not blame him so much as the commanders.° 385
All of a city is in the hands of its leaders,
and likewise an army; those men who lack discipline
become bad through the instruction of their superiors.
This is the whole tale. May he that hates the Atridae
be as dear in the gods' sight as he is in mine. 390

CHORUS [*singing*]
STROPHE
Earth, Mountain Mother, sustainer of all,
mother of Zeus himself,
you who dwell by the great golden Pactolus,
then too, I called on you, revered Mother, 395
when all the insolence of the Atridae assaulted our lord,
O blessed one,
who rides the bull-killing lions,
when they gave his father's weapons, that wonder of the world, 400
to the son of Laertes.

PHILOCTETES [*speaking*]
You have sailed here, as it seems, with a clear tally;
your half of pain matches that of myself.
What you tell me rings in harmony. I recognize   405
the doings of the Atridae and Odysseus.
I know Odysseus would employ his tongue
on every ill tale, every rascality,
that could be brought to issue in injustice.
This is not at all my wonder, but that great Ajax   410
should stand by, see and allow it to happen.

NEOPTOLEMUS
He is no longer living, sir; never, indeed,
if he were, would they have robbed me of the weapons.

PHILOCTETES
What! Is he, too, dead and gone?

NEOPTOLEMUS
Yes, dead and gone. As such now think of him.   415

PHILOCTETES
But not the son of Tydeus nor Odysseus
whom Sisyphus once sold to Laertes!
They will not die; for they should not be living.

NEOPTOLEMUS
Of course, they are not dead; you may be sure
that they are in their glory among the Greeks.   420

PHILOCTETES
What of an old and honest man, my friend,
Nestor of Pylos? Is he alive? He might
have checked their mischief by his wise advice.

NEOPTOLEMUS
Things have gone badly for him. He has lost
his son Antilochus, who once stood by him.   425

PHILOCTETES

Ah!

You have told me the two deaths that most could hurt.

Alas, what should I look for

when Ajax and Antilochus are dead,

and still Odysseus lives, that in their place

ought to be counted among the dead?   430

NEOPTOLEMUS

He's a cunning wrestler; still, Philoctetes,

even the cunning are sometimes tripped up.

PHILOCTETES

Tell me, by the gods, where was Patroclus,

who was your father's dearest friend?

NEOPTOLEMUS

       Dead, too.

In one short sentence I can tell you this.   435

War never takes a bad man except by chance,

it's always the good men.

PHILOCTETES

     You have said the truth.

So I will ask you of one quite unworthy

but dexterous and clever with his tongue.   440

NEOPTOLEMUS

Whom can you mean except Odysseus?

PHILOCTETES

It is not he: there was a man, Thersites,

who never was content to speak just once,

though no one was for letting him speak at all.

Do you know if he is still alive?

NEOPTOLEMUS

     I did not see him,

but I have heard that he is still alive.   445

PHILOCTETES

He would be; nothing evil ever perishes.
The gods somehow give them most excellent care.
They find their pleasure in turning back from Hades
the villains and tricksters, but the just and good
they are always sending out of the world.   450
How can I reckon the score, how can I praise,
when in praising gods' actions° I find these gods are bad?

NEOPTOLEMUS

For my own part, Philoctetes of Oeta,
from now on I shall take precautions.
I shall look at Troy and the Atridae both   455
from very far off. I shall never abide
the company of those where the worse man
has more power than the better, where the good
are always depleted and instead cowards rule.
For the future, rocky Scyrus will content me
to take my pleasure at home.   460
Now I will be going to my ship. Philoctetes,
good-bye, and best wishes. May the gods
relieve you of your sickness, as you would have it!
Let us go, men, that when god grants us sailing
we may be ready to sail.   465

PHILOCTETES

                    Boy, are you going,
    already?

NEOPTOLEMUS

                    Yes, we must not miss our chance
    to sail; we must be ready, not far afield.

PHILOCTETES

My son—I beg you in your father's name,
and in your mother's, in the name of all
that you have loved at home, do not leave me here   470
alone, living in sufferings you have seen

and others you have heard about from me.
I am not your main concern; but give me some passing
    thought.
I know that there is horrible discomfort
in having me on board. But put up with it.
To noble people, as you know, all meanness
is detested, while generosity brings glory.   475
If you leave me here, it is an ugly reproach;
but if you take me, much glory will be your reward,
if I shall live to see the land of Oeta.
Come! One day, hardly one whole day's space   480
that I shall trouble you. Endure this much.
Take me and put me where you will,
in the bilges, in the prow or stern, anywhere
where I shall least offend those that I sail with.
By Zeus himself, god of suppliants,
I beg you, boy, say "Yes," say you will do it!   485
Here I am on my knees to you, helpless,
a poor, lame man. Do not cast me away
so utterly alone, where no one ever walks by.
Either take me and set me safe in your own home,
or take me to Chalcodon's house in Euboea.
From there it will be no great journey for me   490
to Oeta and the ridge of Trachis and
the quick-flowing Spercheius,
so you can show me to my loving father.
For many a day I have feared that he is dead;
I sent messages with those who came to my island,   495
many of them, begging him to come
and bring me home himself. Either he's dead,
or, as I rather think, those messengers
made little of what I asked them, and just hurried home.
Now in you I have found both escort and messenger;   500
bring me safe home. Take pity on me.
Look how men live, always precariously
balanced between good and bad fortune.

If you are out of trouble, watch for danger.
And when you live well, then be most on guard   505
for your life, lest ruin take it unawares.

CHORUS [*singing*]

ANTISTROPHE

Have pity on him, my lord.
He has told us of a most desperate ordeal;
may such things never overtake friends of mine.
And, lord, if you hate the heartless Atridae,   510
I would set their ill treatment of him
to his gain and would carry him   515
in your quick, well-fitted ship
to his home and so avoid offense before the gods.

NEOPTOLEMUS

Take care that your assent is not too ready,
and that, when you have enough of his diseased company,   520
you're no longer consistent with what you've said just now.

CHORUS LEADER

No. You'll never be able to reproach me about this with
    justice.

NEOPTOLEMUS

            I should be ashamed
to be less ready than you to render a stranger service.   525
Well, if you will then, let us sail. Let him
get ready quickly. My ship will carry him.
May the gods give us a safe clearance from this land
and a safe journey where we choose to go.

PHILOCTETES

God bless this day!   530
Man, dear to my very heart,
and you, dear sailors, how shall I prove to you
how you have bound me to your friendship!
Let us go, boy. But let us first kiss the earth,

reverently, in my homeless home of a cave.
I would have you know what I have lived from, 535
how tough the spirit that did not break. I think
the sight itself would have been too much for anyone
except myself. Necessity has taught me,
little by little, to suffer and be patient.

CHORUS LEADER

Wait! Let us see. Two men are coming.
One of them is of our crew, the other a foreigner. 540
Let us hear from them and then go in.

(Enter the Sailor from the side, disguised as a
Merchant, along with another sailor.)

MERCHANT

Son of Achilles, I told my companion here—
he with two others was guarding your ship—
to tell me where you were. I just happened on them; 545
I had no intentions this way. Just by accident
I came to anchor at this island.
I am sailing in command of a ship outward-bound
from Ilium, with no great company, for Peparethus—
a good country, that, for wine. When I heard
that all those sailors were the crew of your ship, 550
I thought I should not hold my tongue and sail on
until I spoke with you—and got my fair reward.
I guess you know nothing about your own affairs
and the Greeks' new plans for you—indeed, not just plans, 555
but actions in train already and not slowly.

NEOPTOLEMUS

Thank you for your consideration, sir.
I will remain obliged to your kindness
unless I prove unworthy. Please tell me
what you have spoken of. I would like to know
what are these new plans of the Greeks. 560

MERCHANT

Old Phoenix and the two sons of Theseus are gone,
pursuing you with a squadron.

NEOPTOLEMUS

Do they intend
to bring me back with violence or persuade me?

MERCHANT

I do not know. I tell you what I heard.

NEOPTOLEMUS

Are Phoenix and his companions so eager   565
to do this as a favor to the two Atridae?

MERCHANT

It is being done.
There is no delay about it. That you should know.

NEOPTOLEMUS

How is it that Odysseus was not ready
to sail as his own messenger on such
an errand? It cannot be he was afraid?

MERCHANT

When I weighed anchor, he and Tydeus' son   570
were setting off in pursuit of another man.

NEOPTOLEMUS

Who was this other man that Odysseus himself should seek
him?

MERCHANT

There was a man—perhaps you will tell me first
who this is; and say softly what you say.

NEOPTOLEMUS

This, sir, is the famous Philoctetes.   575

MERCHANT

                    Do not
ask me any further questions. Get yourself out,
as quickly as you can, out of this island.

PHILOCTETES

What does he say, boy? Why in dark whispers
does he bargain with you about me, this sailor?

NEOPTOLEMUS

I do not know yet what he says, but he must say it,   580
openly, whatever it is, to you and me and these.

MERCHANT

Son of Achilles, do not slander me
to the army for speaking about things I shouldn't.
There's many a thing I do for them and in return
get something from them, as a poor man may.

NEOPTOLEMUS

I am the enemy of the Atridae; and this man   585
is my greatest friend because he hates them too.
You have come to me as a friend, and so you must
hide from us nothing that you heard.

MERCHANT

Well, watch what you are doing, sir.

NEOPTOLEMUS

                    I have been careful
all along.

MERCHANT

        I shall put the whole responsibility
squarely upon you.   590

NEOPTOLEMUS

                    Do so; but speak.

MERCHANT

        Well, then. The two I have spoken of,

the son of Tydeus and the mighty Odysseus,
are in pursuit of this man here.
They have sworn by the gods to bring him back with them
either by persuasion or by brute force.
And this all the Greeks heard clearly announced   595
by lord Odysseus; for he was much more confident
of success than was the other.

NEOPTOLEMUS
                              What can have made
the Atridae care about him after so long—
one whom they, years and years since, cast away?   600
What yearning for him came over them? Was it the gods
who punish evil doings that now have driven them
to retribution for injustice?

MERCHANT
I will explain all that. Perhaps you haven't heard.
There was a prophet of very good family,
a son of Priam indeed, called Helenus.   605
He was captured one night in an expedition
undertaken single-handed by Odysseus,
of whom all base and shameful things are spoken,
captured by stratagem. Odysseus brought
his prisoner before the Greeks, a splendid prize.
Helenus prophesied everything to them   610
and, in particular, concerning the fortress of Troy,
that they could never take it till they persuaded
Philoctetes to come with them and leave his island.
As soon as Odysseus heard the prophet say this,   615
he promised at once to bring the man before them,
for all to see—he thought, as a willing prisoner,
but, if not that, against his will. And if he failed,
"any of them might have his head," he declared. My boy,
that is the whole story; that is why I urge you   620
and him and any that you care for to make haste.

PHILOCTETES

Ah!

Did he indeed swear that he would persuade me
to rejoin the Achaeans, did he so, that utter devil?
As soon shall I be persuaded, when I am dead,
to rise from Hades' house and come to the light again,   625
as his own father did.

MERCHANT

I do not know about that. Well, I will be going now
to my ship. May god prosper you both!

                    (Exit Merchant to the side with the other sailor.)

PHILOCTETES

Is it not shocking, boy, that the son of Laertes
should think that there are words soft enough to win me,
to let him put me in his boat, exhibit me
in front of all the Greeks?   630
No! I would rather listen to my worst enemy,
the snake that bit me, made me thus lame and useless.
But he will say anything; he will dare anything;
and now I know that he will come here.
Boy, let us go, that a great expanse of sea   635
may separate us from Odysseus' ship.
Let us go. For you know, swift action in due season
brings rest and peace when once the work is done.

NEOPTOLEMUS

When the wind at our prow falls, we can sail, no sooner.
Now it is dead against us.   640

PHILOCTETES

It is always fair sailing, when you're escaping evil.

NEOPTOLEMUS

Yes, but the wind is against them, too.

PHILOCTETES

                              For pirates
when they can thieve and plunder, no wind is contrary.

NEOPTOLEMUS

If you will, then, let us go. Take from your cave   645
what you need most and love most.

PHILOCTETES

There are some things I need, but no great choice.

NEOPTOLEMUS

What is there that you will not find on board?

PHILOCTETES

An herb I have, the chief means to soothe my wound,
to lull the pain to sleep.   650

NEOPTOLEMUS

                              Bring it out then.
What else is there that you would have?

PHILOCTETES

                              Any arrow
I may have dropped and missed. For none of them
must I leave for anyone else to pick up.

NEOPTOLEMUS

Is this, in your hands, the famous bow?

PHILOCTETES

                    Yes, this,   655
this in my hands.

NEOPTOLEMUS

                    May I see it closer,
touch and kiss it like a god?

PHILOCTETES

                              For you, this will be granted,
and anything else of mine that is for your good.

NEOPTOLEMUS

I long for it, yet only with such longing   660
that if it is allowed, I may have it, else let it be.

PHILOCTETES

    Your words are holy, boy. It is allowed,
for you have given me the sunlight,
the sight of the sun shining above us here,
a hope to see my Oeta, my old father, my friends.   665
You have raised me up above my enemies,
when I was under their feet. You may be assured:
you may indeed touch my bow, then give it back
to me that gave it you—and proclaim that alone
of all the world you touched it, in return
for the good deed you did. It was for that,
for friendly help, I myself won it first.   670

NEOPTOLEMUS

    I am glad to see you and take you as a friend.
For one who knows how to show and to accept kindness
will be a friend better than any possession.
Go in.

PHILOCTETES

    I will bring you with me. The sickness in me
needs to have you beside me.   675

        (*Neoptolemus and Philoctetes enter the cave together.*)

CHORUS [*singing*]

        STROPHE A

In story I have heard, but my eyes have not seen
him that once came near to Zeus's marriage bed:
I have heard how Zeus, son of Cronus, invincible,
caught him, bound him on a turning wheel.
But I know of no other,   680
whether by hearsay or by sight, of all mankind
who ever met with a destiny more hateful
than Philoctetes', who wronged no one, nor killed,
but lived, a just man among the just,
yet fell into misery quite undeservedly.   685
There is wonder, indeed, in my heart

how, how in his loneliness,
listening to the waves beating on the shore,
how he kept hold at all
on a life so full of tears.   690

He was lame, and no one came near him.
He suffered, and there were no neighbors for his sorrow
with whom his cries would find answer,
with whom he could lament the bloody plague
that ate him up.   695
No one who would gather
fallen leaves from the ground
to quiet the raging, bleeding sore,
running, in his maggot-rotten foot.   700
Here and there he crawled
writhing always—
suffering like a child
without the nurse he loves—
to whatever source of ease he could find   705
when the heart-devouring suffering relented.

No grain sown in holy earth was his, nor other food
of all enjoyed by us, men who live by labor,
save when with the feathered arrows shot by the quick bow   710
he got himself food for his belly.
Ah, poor soul,
that never in ten years' length
enjoyed a drink of wine   715
but looked always for standing pools of water
and tried to approach them.

But now he will end fortunate. He has fallen in
with the son of good men. He will be great, after it all.   720
Our prince in his seagoing craft will carry him
after the fullness of many months, to his father's home

in the country of the Malian nymphs,   725
by the banks of the Spercheius,
where the hero of the bronze shield ascended
to all the gods, ablaze in holy fire
above the ridges of Oeta.

(Neoptolemus and Philoctetes reenter from the cave.)

NEOPTOLEMUS
Come if you will, then. Why have you nothing to say?   730
Why do you stand like that, in silence transfixed?

PHILOCTETES
Oh! Oh!

NEOPTOLEMUS
What is it?

PHILOCTETES
Nothing to be afraid of. Come on, boy.

NEOPTOLEMUS
Is it the pain of your inveterate sickness?

PHILOCTETES
No, no, indeed not. Just now I think I feel better.   735
O gods!

NEOPTOLEMUS
Why do you call on the gods with cries of distress?

PHILOCTETES
That they may come as healers, come with gentleness.
Oh! Oh! Oh!

NEOPTOLEMUS
What ails you? Tell me; do not keep silence.   740
You are clearly in some pain.

PHILOCTETES
                              I am lost, boy.
I will not be able to hide it from you longer.

Oh! Oh!
It goes through me, right through me!
Miserable, miserable!
I am lost, boy. I am being eaten up. Ah!   745
By the gods, if you have a sword, ready to hand, use it!
Strike the end of my foot. Cut it off, I tell you, now.
Do not spare my life. Quick, boy, quick.   750

NEOPTOLEMUS
What is this thing that comes upon you suddenly,
that makes you cry and shriek so?

PHILOCTETES
                    You know, my son!

NEOPTOLEMUS
What is it?

PHILOCTETES
                    You know, boy, surely!

NEOPTOLEMUS
                    What do you mean?
I do not know.

PHILOCTETES
                    You surely know. Oh! Oh!

NEOPTOLEMUS
The terrible burden of your sickness.   755

PHILOCTETES
Terrible it is, beyond words' reach. But pity me.

NEOPTOLEMUS
What shall I do?

PHILOCTETES
                    Do not be afraid and leave me.
It always comes back after a while, I suppose when it's had
its fill of wandering in other places—my affliction.

NEOPTOLEMUS

You most unhappy man,
you that have endured all agonies, lived through them,   760
shall I take hold of you? Shall I touch you?

PHILOCTETES

No, not that, please! But take this bow,
as you asked to do just now, until the pain
of my sickness now upon me has grown less.   765
Keep the bow, guard it safely. Sleep comes upon me
when this affliction departs. There is no relief until then.
But you must let me sleep quietly;
and if they should come in the time when I'm asleep,
by the gods I beg you do not give up my bow   770
willingly or unwillingly to anyone;
and let no one trick you out of it, lest you prove
a murderer—your own and mine, who supplicate you.

NEOPTOLEMUS

I shall take care; be easy about that. It shall not pass
except to your hands and to mine. Give it to me now,
and may good luck go with it!   775

PHILOCTETES

                    Here,
take it, boy. Make a prayer to the gods' envy
that the bow may not be to you a sorrow,
as it was to me and to its former master.

NEOPTOLEMUS

You gods, grant us this; and grant us too
a journey speedy with a prosperous wind   780
to where god sends us and our voyage holds.

PHILOCTETES

Ah! Ah!
An empty prayer, I am afraid, boy:
the blood is trickling, dripping murderously

from its deep spring. I look for something new.
It is coming now, coming.   785
Ah!
You know my condition. Do not leave me now.
Ah!
O man of Cephallenia, if only it were you,
whose chest these pains transfix right through.
Ah!   790
          O Agamemnon and Menelaus, you two generals,
if only it were your two bodies that had fed   795
this sickness for as long as mine has. Ah!

Death, death, how is it that I can call on you,
always, day in, day out, and you cannot come to me?
Boy, my good boy, take up this body of mine
and burn it on what they call the Lemnian fire.   800
I had the resolution once to do this for another,
the son of Zeus, and so obtained the arms
that you now hold. What do you say?
What do you say? Nothing? Where are you, boy?   805

NEOPTOLEMUS

I have been in pain for you; I have long been
in sorrow for your pain.

PHILOCTETES

No, boy, keep up your heart. It is quick in coming
and quick to go. Only I entreat you, do not
leave me alone.

NEOPTOLEMUS

Do not be afraid. We shall stay.   810

PHILOCTETES

You will?

NEOPTOLEMUS

You may be sure of it.

PHILOCTETES

Your oath,
I do not think I need to put you to your oath.

NEOPTOLEMUS

No, it wouldn't be right for me go without you.

PHILOCTETES

Give me your hand upon it.

NEOPTOLEMUS

Here I give it you,
to remain.

PHILOCTETES

Now—take me away from here—

NEOPTOLEMUS

What do you mean?

PHILOCTETES

Up, up.

NEOPTOLEMUS

What madness is upon you? Why do you look   815
to the sky above us?

PHILOCTETES

Let me go, let me go.

NEOPTOLEMUS

Where?

PHILOCTETES

Oh, let me go.

NEOPTOLEMUS

Not I.

PHILOCTETES

You will kill me if you touch me.

NEOPTOLEMUS

Now I shall let you go, now you are calmer.

PHILOCTETES

Earth, take my body, dying as I am.
The pain no longer lets me stand.   820

NEOPTOLEMUS

In a little while, I think,
sleep will come on this man. His head is nodding.
The sweat is soaking all his body over,
and a black flux of blood and matter has broken
out of his foot. Let us leave him quiet, friends,   825
until he falls asleep.

CHORUS [singing]

STROPHE

Sleep that knows not pain nor suffering
kindly, lord, for us,
kindly, kindly come.
Spread your enveloping radiance,   830
as now, over his eyes.
Come, come, Lord Healer.
Boy, look to where you stand,
and where you are going; look to your plans
for the future. Do you see? He sleeps.
What is it we are waiting to do?   835
The critical moment that holds decision over all things
wins many a victory suddenly.

NEOPTOLEMUS [singing]

Yes, it is true he hears nothing, but I see we have hunted in vain,
vainly have captured our quarry the bow, if we sail without him.   840
His is the crown of victory, him the god said we must bring.
Shame shall be ours if we boast and our lies still leave victory
    unwon.

CHORUS

ANTISTROPHE

Boy, to all of this the god shall look.
Answer me gently;
low, low, whisper, whisper, boy.   845
The sleep of a sick man has keen eyes.
It is a sleep unsleeping.
But to the limits of what you can,
look to this, look to this secretly,   850
how you may do it.
You know of whom I speak.
If your mind holds the same purpose touching this man,
the wise can see trouble and no way to cure it.°

EPODE

It is a fair wind, boy, a fair wind: 855
the man is eyeless and helpless,
outstretched under night's blanket—
asleep in the sun is good—
neither of foot nor of hand nor of anything is he master,   860
but is even as one that lies in Death's house.
Look to it, look if what you say
fits the moment. As far as my mind,
boy, can grasp it, best is the trouble taken
that causes the least fear.

NEOPTOLEMUS [*speaking*]

Quiet, I tell you! Are you mad? He is stirring,   865
his eyes are opening; he is raising his head.

PHILOCTETES

Blessed the light that comes after my sleep,
blessed the watching of friends.
I never would have hoped this, my boy,
that you would have the pity of heart to support   870
my afflictions, that you should stand by me and help.
The Atridae, those brave generals, were not so,

they could not so easily put up with me.
You have a noble nature, Neoptolemus,
and noble were your parents. You have made light   875
of all of this—the offense of my cries and the stench.
And now, since it would seem my sickness
can forget me for a while and rest, raise me yourself,
raise me up, boy, and set me on my feet,
so that when my weariness releases me,
we can go to the ship and sail without delay.   880

NEOPTOLEMUS
I am glad to see you unexpectedly,
eyes open, free of pain, still with the breath of life.
In watching you suffer so, all the signs pointed
to your being no more. Now, lift yourself up.   885
If you would rather, these men will lift you. They
will spare no trouble, since you and I are agreed.

PHILOCTETES
Thanks, boy. Lift me yourself, as you thought of it.
Do not trouble them, let them not be disquieted   890
before they need by the foul smell of me; living
on board with me will try their patience enough.

NEOPTOLEMUS
Very well, then; stand up; take hold of me yourself.

PHILOCTETES
Do not be afraid; old habit will help me up.

NEOPTOLEMUS
Ah! What shall I do from now on?   895

PHILOCTETES
What is it, boy? Where are your words straying?

NEOPTOLEMUS
I do not know what to say. I am at a loss.

PHILOCTETES

Why are you at a loss? Do not say so, boy.

NEOPTOLEMUS

But this is where I've come to in this ordeal.

PHILOCTETES

Is it disgust at my sickness? Is it this   900
that makes you shrink from taking me?

NEOPTOLEMUS

All is disgust when someone leaves his own nature
and does things that are unlike him.

PHILOCTETES

But it is not unlike your father, either in word
or in act, to help a good man.   905

NEOPTOLEMUS

I shall be seen to be dishonorable:
that's what has been causing me pain.

PHILOCTETES

Not in your present actions. But your words make me
    hesitate.

NEOPTOLEMUS

Zeus, what must I do? Twice be proved rotten,
hiding what I shouldn't, saying what is most foul?

PHILOCTETES

Unless I am wrong, here is a man who will   910
betray me, leave me—so it seems—and sail away.

NEOPTOLEMUS

Not I; I will not leave you. But to your bitterness,
I might send you on a journey—and that's what I'm
    pained by.

PHILOCTETES

What are you saying, boy? I do not understand.

NEOPTOLEMUS

I will not hide anything. You must sail to Troy   915
to the Achaeans, join the army of the Atridae.

PHILOCTETES

What! What can you mean?

NEOPTOLEMUS

                              Do not cry yet
until you learn.

PHILOCTETES

Learn what? What would you do with me?

NEOPTOLEMUS

First save you from this torture, then with you
together go and lay waste the land of Troy.   920

PHILOCTETES

                              You would?
This is, in truth, what you intend?

NEOPTOLEMUS

                              Necessity,
a great necessity compels it. Do not be angry.

PHILOCTETES

Then I am lost. I am betrayed. Why, stranger,
have you done this to me? Give me back my bow.

NEOPTOLEMUS

That I cannot. Justice and interest   925
make me obedient to those in authority.

PHILOCTETES

You fire, you every horror, most hateful engine
of ruthless mischief, what have you done to me,
what treachery! Have you no shame to see me
that kneeled to you, entreated you, hard of heart?   930
You robbed me of my life, taking my bow.

Give it back, I beg you, give it back, I pray, my boy!
By your father's gods, do not take my life.

He does not say a word,
but turns away his eyes. He will not give it up.   935

Harbors and headlands, dens of wild creatures,
you jutting broken crags, to you I raise my cry—
there is no one else that I can speak to—
and you have always been there, have always heard me:
let me tell you what he has done to me, this boy,   940
Achilles' son. He swore to bring me home;
he brings me to Troy. He gave me his right hand,
then took and keeps my sacred bow,
the bow of Heracles, the son of Zeus,
and means to show me off to the Argives,
as though in me he had conquered a strong man
by force.   945
He does not know he is killing one that is dead,
a kind of vaporous shadow, a mere wraith.
Had I had my strength, he would not have conquered me,
for, even as I am, it was trickery that did it.
I have been deceived and am lost.
What can I do?
Give it back. Be your true self again. Will you not?   950
No word. Then I am nothing.

Two doors cut in the rock, to you again,
I come, but now unarmed, and all without
the means to feed myself! Here in this hovel
I shall shrivel to death alone. I shall kill no more
the winged bird nor wild thing of the hills   955
with that bow of mine. I shall myself in death
be a feast for those that fed me. Those that I hunted
shall be my hunters now.
Life for the life I took, I shall repay
at the hands of this man that seemed to know no harm.   960

My curse upon your life!—but not yet still
until I know if you will change again;
if you will not, may an evil death be yours!

CHORUS LEADER

What shall we do? Shall we sail? Shall we do as he asks?
Prince, it is you must decide.

NEOPTOLEMUS

A kind of compassion,   965
a terrible compassion, has come upon me
for him. I've been feeling it long since, more and more.

PHILOCTETES

Pity me, boy, by the gods; do not bring on yourself
men's blame for your crafty victory over me.

NEOPTOLEMUS

What shall I do? I wish I had never left
Scyrus, so hateful is what I face now.   970

PHILOCTETES

You are not bad yourself; by bad men's teaching
you came to practice your foul lesson. Now leave it to others
such as it suits, and sail away. Give me my weapons.

NEOPTOLEMUS

What shall we do, men?

(Enter Odysseus from the side.)

ODYSSEUS

You fool, what are you doing?
Hand that bow over to me, and back off!   975

PHILOCTETES

Who is this? Is that Odysseus' voice?

ODYSSEUS

                                        It is.
Odysseus certainly; you can see me here.

PHILOCTETES

Then I've been sold out indeed; I am lost. It was he
who took me prisoner, robbed me of my weapons.

ODYSSEUS

Yes, I, I and no other. I admit that.   980

PHILOCTETES

Boy, give me back my bow, give it back to me.

ODYSSEUS

That he will never
be able to do now, even if he wishes it.
And you must come with the bow, or else these men
will take you by force.

PHILOCTETES

Me? Your wickedness and impudence are without limit.
Will these men really take me there by force?   985

ODYSSEUS

Yes, if you do not come of your own accord.

PHILOCTETES

O land of Lemnos and all-mastering brightness,
Hephaestus-fashioned, must I indeed bear this,
that he, Odysseus, drags me from you with violence?

ODYSSEUS

It is Zeus, I would have you know, Zeus this land's ruler,
who has determined. I am only his servant.   990

PHILOCTETES

Hateful creature,
what excuses you invent! You plead the gods
to screen your actions and make the gods out liars.

ODYSSEUS

They speak the truth. The road must be traveled.

PHILOCTETES

I say No.

ODYSSEUS

    I say Yes. You must listen.

PHILOCTETES

    Am I after all a slave, not free? Is that   995
    what my father sired me to be?

ODYSSEUS

                  No, but to be equal
    of the best, with whom it is destined you must take Troy,
    and demolish her stone by stone.

PHILOCTETES

    Never—I would rather suffer anything than this.
    There is still my steep and rugged precipice here.   1000

ODYSSEUS

    What do you mean to do?

PHILOCTETES

                  Throw myself down,
    shatter my head upon the rock below.

ODYSSEUS

    Hold him. Take this solution out of his power.

PHILOCTETES

    Hands of mine, prey of Odysseus' hunting,
    how you suffer now in your lack of the loved bowstring!   1005

    You who have never had a healthy thought
    nor a noble one, you Odysseus, how you have hunted me,
    how you have stolen upon me with this boy
    as your shield, because I did not know him, one
    that is no mate for you but worthy of me,
    who knew nothing but to do what he was bidden,   1010
    and now, you see, is suffering bitterly
    for his own faults and the evils brought on me.
    Your sneaky, dark-plotting soul taught him step by step

to be clever in mischief against his nature and will.   1015
Now it is my turn; now to my sorrow you intend
to tie me hand and foot and take me away,
away from this shore on which you cast me once
without friends or comrades or city, a dead man among the
   living.
Ah!
My curse on you! I have often cursed you before,
yet the gods give me nothing that is sweet to me;   1020
so you have joy in living, and I have sorrow
because my very life is linked to this pain,
laughed at by you and your two generals,
the sons of Atreus whom you serve in this.
And yet, when you sailed with them, it was by constraint   1025
and trickery, while I came of my own free will
with seven ships, to my undoing, I
who was then dishonored and cast away—
you say it was they that did it; but they say you.
     But now why are you taking me? For what?
I am nothing now. To you all I have long been dead.   1030
You god-hated wretch, how is it that no longer
am I lame and foul-smelling to you? How can you sacrifice
to the gods if I sail with you? Pour your libations?
This was your excuse for casting me away.
May death in ugly form come on you! It will so come,   1035
since you have wronged me, if the gods care for justice.
And I know that they do care for it, for otherwise
you never would have sailed here for my sake
and my future, had not the divine goad,
a need of me, compelled you.
     Land of my fathers, gods that look on men's deeds,   1040
take vengeance on these men, late but at last,
upon them all, if you have pity on me!
Wretchedly as I live, if I saw them
dead, I could think that I was free of my sickness.

CHORUS LEADER

He is a hard man, Odysseus, this stranger,   1045
and hard his words: no yielding to suffering in them.

ODYSSEUS

If I had the time, I have much I could say to him.
As it is, there is only one thing. As the occasion
demands, such a one am I.
When there is a competition of men just and good,   1050
you will find none more scrupulous than myself.
What I seek in everything is to win—
except in your regard: I willingly yield to you now.

Let him go, men. Do not lay a finger on him.
Let him stay here. We have these weapons of yours   1055
and do not need you, Philoctetes.
Teucer is with us who has the skill and I,
who, I think, am no inferior master of them
and have as straight an aim as you. Why do we need you?
Farewell: keep walking around Lemnos. Let us go.   1060
Perhaps your prize will bring me the honor you should
   have had.

PHILOCTETES

Oh! What shall I do? Will you appear
before the Argives in the glory of my weapons?

ODYSSEUS

Say nothing further to me. I am going.   1065

PHILOCTETES

Son of Achilles, your voice has no word for me?
Will you go away in silence?

ODYSSEUS

                              Come, Neoptolemus.
Do not look at him. Your generosity
may spoil our future.

PHILOCTETES

    You, too, men, will you go   1070
and leave me alone? Do you, too, have no pity?

CHORUS LEADER

This young man is our captain. What he says to you
we say as well.

NEOPTOLEMUS   (To the Chorus.)

    Odysseus will tell me
that I am too full of pity. Still
remain, if this man will have it so, as long   1075
as it takes the sailors to ready the ship
and until we have made our prayer to the gods.
Perhaps, in the meantime, he will have better thoughts
about us. Let us go, Odysseus.
You, when we call you, be quick to come.   1080

            (Exit Odysseus and Neoptolemus to the side.)

PHILOCTETES [singing, while the Chorus sings in reply]

STROPHE A

Hollow cave in the rock, sun-warmed, ice-cold,
I was not destined, after all, ever to leave you.
Still with me, you shall be witness to my dying.   1085
Passageway, crowded with my cries of pain,
what shall be, now again, my daily life with you?
What hope shall I find of food to keep my wretched life alive?   1090
Come close now, birds that once were so timid,
come down the shrill winds; I no longer have strength to
    catch you.

CHORUS

It was you who doomed yourself,   1095
man of hard fortune. From no other,
from nothing stronger, came your mischance.
When you could have chosen wisdom,
with better opportunity before you,
you chose the worse.   1100

PHILOCTETES

Sorrow, sorrow is mine. Suffering has broken me,
who must live henceforth alone from all the world,
must live here and die here;   1105
no longer bringing home food nor winning
it with winged weapons and strong hands.   1110
Unnoticed, the crafty words of a treacherous mind
stole up on me. Would I might see him,
contriver of this trap,
for as long as I am, condemned to pain.   1115

CHORUS

It was the will of the gods
that has subdued you, no trickery
to which my hand was lent.   1120
Turn your hate, your ill-omened curses, elsewhere.
This indeed lies near my heart,
that you should not reject my friendship.   1125

PHILOCTETES

By the shore of the gray sea he sits and laughs at me.
He brandishes in his hand the weapon which kept me alive,
which no one else had handled. Bow that I loved,
forced from the hands that loved you, if you could feel,
you would see me with pity, successor to Heracles,   1130
that used you and shall handle you no more.
You have found a new master, a man of craft,   1135
and shall be bent by him.
You shall see crooked deceits and the face of my hateful foe,
and a thousand ill things such as he contrived against me.

CHORUS

A man should give careful heed to speak his own right;°   1140
and when he has said it, restrain his tongue from rancor and
    taunt.

Odysseus was one man, one out of many;
appointed by his commander he did this, a service to his friends.   1145

PHILOCTETES

ANTISTROPHE B

Birds my victims, and tribes of bright-eyed wild creatures,
tenants of these hills, no longer need you flee from me or my house.
No more do I have the strength of my hands, of my bow.   1150
Come! I'm lame, you have nothing to fear.°
It is a good time   1155
to glut yourselves freely on my discolored flesh.
For shortly I shall die here. How shall I find means of life?
Who can live on air without any of all that life-giving earth
     supplies?   1160

CHORUS

In the name of the gods, if there is anything that you hold in
     respect,
draw near to a friend that approaches you in all sincerity.
Know what you are doing, know it well.
It lies with you to avoid this doom.   1165
To feed it with your body is a pitiable destiny;
and he who dwells with it can never learn
how to endure the thousand agonies.

PHILOCTETES

EPODE

Again, again you have touched my old hurt,   1170
for all that you are the best of those that came here.
Why did you afflict me? What have you done to me?

CHORUS

What do you mean by this?

PHILOCTETES

You have hoped to bring me
to the hateful land of Troy.   1175

CHORUS

I judge that to be best.

PHILOCTETES

Then leave me now at once.

CHORUS

Glad news, glad news you give me.
I am right willing to obey you.
Let us go now to our places in the ship.　　　　　　　1180

PHILOCTETES

No, by Zeus who listens to curses, do not go,
I beseech you.

CHORUS

Be calm!

PHILOCTETES

　　　　　　　　　　　　Friends, stay!
I beg you to stay.　　　　　　　　　　　　　　　1185

CHORUS

　　　　　　Why do you call on us?

PHILOCTETES

Ah, ah!
It is the spirit that haunts me. I am destroyed.
My foot, what shall I do with this foot of mine
in the life I shall live hereafter?　　　　　　　　　1190
Friends, come to me again.

CHORUS

What to do? Your wishes now are different
from your former bidding.

PHILOCTETES

It is no occasion for anger
when a man crazy with storms of pain
speaks contrary to reason.　　　　　　　　　　　　1195

CHORUS

Unhappy man, come with us, as we say.

PHILOCTETES

    Never, never! That is my fixed purpose.
    Not though the lord of the lightning, bearing his fiery bolts,
    come against me, burning me
    with flame and glare.
    Let Ilium go to hell and all those that under its walls   1200
    had the heart to cast me away, crippled!
    Friends, grant me one prayer only.

CHORUS

                     What is it you would seek?

PHILOCTETES

    A sword, if you have got one,
    or an axe or some weapon—give it me!   1205

CHORUS

    What would you do with it?

PHILOCTETES

                 Head and foot,
    head and foot, all of me, I would cut with my own hand.
    My mind is set on death, on death, I tell you.

CHORUS

    Why this?   1210

PHILOCTETES

    I would go seek my father.

CHORUS

    Where?

PHILOCTETES

             In the house of Hades.
    He is no longer in the light.
    City of my fathers, if only I could see you!
    I, wretched man that I am, left your holy streams,   1215
    to go help the Greeks, my enemies,
    and now am nothing any more.

CHORUS LEADER [*speaking*]

I should have been by now on my way to the ship,°
if I did not see Odysseus coming here   1220
and with him the son of Achilles.

> (*Enter Odysseus and Neoptolemus from the side.*
> *Philoctetes withdraws into the cave.*)

ODYSSEUS

You have turned back; there is hurry in your step.
Will you not tell me why?

NEOPTOLEMUS

I am hurrying to undo the wrong that I have done.

ODYSSEUS

A strange thing to say! What wrong was that?   1225

NEOPTOLEMUS

I did wrong when I obeyed you and the Greeks.

ODYSSEUS

What did you do that you think was unworthy?

NEOPTOLEMUS

I caught a man with tricks and with treachery.

ODYSSEUS

What man? Ah, do you have something rash in mind?

NEOPTOLEMUS

Nothing rash. But to the son of Poias . . .   1230

ODYSSEUS

What? I am afraid to hear what you will say.

NEOPTOLEMUS

Back to the man I took it from, this bow . . .

ODYSSEUS

You cannot mean you are going to give it back.

NEOPTOLEMUS

Just that. To my shame, unjustly I obtained it.

ODYSSEUS

By the gods, you speak in earnest?   1235

NEOPTOLEMUS

                    Yes, unless
it is not in earnest to tell you the truth.

ODYSSEUS

What do you mean, son of Achilles, what are you saying?

NEOPTOLEMUS

Must I tell you the same story twice or thrice?

ODYSSEUS

I should prefer not to have heard it once.

NEOPTOLEMUS

You can rest easy. You have now heard everything.   1240

ODYSSEUS

Then there is someone who will prevent its execution.

NEOPTOLEMUS

Who will that be? Who will stop me?

ODYSSEUS

The whole assembly
of the Greeks and among them I myself.

NEOPTOLEMUS

You are a clever man, Odysseus, but
this is not a clever thing to say.

ODYSSEUS

                In your own case
neither the words nor the acts are clever.   1245

NEOPTOLEMUS

                              Still
if they are just, that's better than being clever.

ODYSSEUS

How can it be just to give up and surrender
what you won by my plans?

NEOPTOLEMUS

It was wrong,
a shameful wrong, which I shall try to redeem.

ODYSSEUS

Have you no fear of the Greeks if you do this?   1250

NEOPTOLEMUS

I have no fear of anything you can do,°
when I act with justice; nor shall I yield to force.

ODYSSEUS

Then we shall be fighting
not with the Trojans but with you.

NEOPTOLEMUS

Let that be as it will.

ODYSSEUS

Do you see my hand,
reaching for the sword?   1255

NEOPTOLEMUS

You shall see me do the same
and with no hesitation!

ODYSSEUS

I will let you alone;
I shall go and tell this to the assembled Greeks,
and they will punish you.

NEOPTOLEMUS

That is very prudent.
If you are always as prudent as this,
perhaps you will keep out of trouble.   1260

(Exit Odysseus to the side.)

Philoctetes, son of Poias, I call on you!
Come out from this rocky home of yours.

(Philoctetes appears at the mouth of the cave.)

PHILOCTETES

What cry is this at the door?
Why do you call me, strangers? What would you have?
Ah! This is a bad thing. Can there be some fresh mischief   1265
you come to do, to top what you have done already?

NEOPTOLEMUS

Be easy. I would only have you listen.

PHILOCTETES

I am afraid of that.
I heard you before, and they were good words, too.
But they destroyed me when I listened.

NEOPTOLEMUS

Is there no place, then, for repentance?   1270

PHILOCTETES

You were just such a one in words when you stole my bow,
inspiring confidence, but sly and treacherous.

NEOPTOLEMUS

I am not such now. But I would hear from you
whether you are entirely determined
to remain here, or will you go with us?   1275

PHILOCTETES

Oh, stop! You need not say another word.
All that you say will be wasted.

NEOPTOLEMUS

You are determined?

PHILOCTETES

                    More than words can declare.

NEOPTOLEMUS

Well, I wish that I could have persuaded you.
But if I cannot speak to some purpose, I have done.

PHILOCTETES

Indeed, you will say it all   1280
to no purpose, for you will never win my heart
to friendship with you, who have stolen my life
by treachery, and then came and lectured me,
most hateful son of a noble father. Cursed be you all,
first the two sons of Atreus, then Odysseus,   1285
and then yourself!

NEOPTOLEMUS

                          Do not curse me any more.
Take your bow. Here I give it to you.

PHILOCTETES

What can you mean? Is this another trick?

NEOPTOLEMUS

No. That I swear by the holy majesty
of Zeus on high!

PHILOCTETES

These are good words,   1290
if only they are honest.

NEOPTOLEMUS

The fact is plain.
Stretch out your hand; take your own bow again.

                              (He hands the bow to Philoctetes. Odysseus
                                     appears suddenly, from the side.)

ODYSSEUS

I forbid it, as the gods are my witnesses,
in the name of the Atridae and the Greeks.

PHILOCTETES

Whose voice is that, boy? Is it Odysseus?   1295

ODYSSEUS

You heard right—and near at hand!
And I shall bring you to the plains of Troy
by force, whether Achilles' son
will have it so or not.

PHILOCTETES   *(Starting to aim at him.)*

You will be sorry for your words
if this arrow flies straight.

NEOPTOLEMUS

No, Philoctetes, no!   1300
Do not shoot.

PHILOCTETES

Let me go, let go my hand, dear boy.

NEOPTOLEMUS

I will not.

(Exit Odysseus to the side.)

PHILOCTETES

Why did you prevent me killing my enemy,
with my bow, a man that hates me?

NEOPTOLEMUS

This is not to our glory, neither yours nor mine.

PHILOCTETES

Well, know this much, that the princes of the army,   1305
the lying heralds of the Greeks, are cowards
when they face real combat, however keen in words.

NEOPTOLEMUS

Let that be. You have your bow. There is no further cause
for anger or reproach against me.

PHILOCTETES
None.

You have shown your nature and true breeding,   1310
son of Achilles and not Sisyphus.
Your father, when he still was with the living,
was the most famous of them all, as now he is of the dead.

NEOPTOLEMUS
I am happy to hear you speak well of my father
and of myself. Now listen to my request.   1315
The fortunes that the gods give to us men
we must bear under necessity.
But men that cling willfully to their sufferings
as you do, no one may forgive nor pity.   1320
Your anger has made a savage of you. You will not
accept advice, although the friend advises
in pure goodheartedness. You loathe him, think
he is your enemy and hates you.
Yet I will speak. May Zeus, the god of oaths,
be my witness! Mark it, Philoctetes, write it in your mind.   1325
You are sick and the pain of the sickness is of divine origin
because you approached the guardian of Chryse,
the serpent that with secret watch protects
her roofless shrine to keep it from violation.
You will never know relief while the selfsame sun   1330
rises on this side and sets again on that,
until you come of your own will to Troy,
and meet among us the sons of Asclepius,
who will relieve your sickness; then with the bow
and by my side, you will become Troy's conqueror.   1335

I will tell you how I know that this is so.
There is a man of Troy who was taken prisoner,
Helenus, a good prophet. He told us clearly
how it should be and said, besides, that Troy   1340
must fall completely this summer. He even says,
"If I prove wrong, you may kill me."

Now since you know this, yield and be gracious.
It is a glorious increase of your gain,
for you, judged preeminent among the Greeks,
first, to come into hands that can heal you,   1345
and then to win the highest renown, by taking
Troy that has cost infinity of tears.

PHILOCTETES

Hateful life, why should I still be alive and seeing?
Why not be gone to Hades?
What shall I do? How can I distrust   1350
his words who in friendship has counseled me?
Shall I then yield? If I do so, how come
before the eyes of men, so miserable?
Who will say word of greeting to me?
Eyes of mine, that have seen all, can you endure   1355
to see me conversing with my murderers,
the sons of Atreus? With cursed Odysseus?
It is not the sting of wrongs past
but what I must look for in wrongs to come.
Men whose wit has been mother of villainy once   1360
have learned from it to be evil in all other things too.°
I must indeed wonder at yourself in this.
You should not yourself be going to Troy,
and you should be holding me back. They've done you wrong
and robbed you of your father's arms.° Will you go   1365
and help them fight, and compel me to do the same?
No, boy, no; take me home as you promised.
Remain in Scyrus yourself; let these bad men
die in their own bad fashion. We shall both thank you,   1370
I and my father. You will not then, by helping
the wicked, seem to be like them.

NEOPTOLEMUS

       What you say
is reasonable; yet I wish that you'd trust the gods
and my word, and so set sail, with me as friend.   1375

PHILOCTETES

What, to the plains of Troy, to the cursed sons
of Atreus with this suffering foot of mine?

NEOPTOLEMUS

To those that shall give you redress,
that shall save you and your rotting foot from its disease.

PHILOCTETES

That's terrible advice: what do you mean by it?   1380

NEOPTOLEMUS

What I see fulfilled will be best for you and me.

PHILOCTETES

And saying it, don't you blush before the gods?

NEOPTOLEMUS

Why should one feel ashamed to do good to another?

PHILOCTETES

Is the good for the Atridae or for me?

NEOPTOLEMUS

I am your friend, and the word I speak is friendly.   1385

PHILOCTETES

How, then, do you wish to betray me to my enemies?

NEOPTOLEMUS

Sir, learn not to be defiant in misfortune.

PHILOCTETES

You will ruin me, I know it, by your words.

NEOPTOLEMUS

Not I. You do not understand, I think.

PHILOCTETES

Do I not know the Atridae cast me away?   1390

NEOPTOLEMUS

They cast you away; see if now they will restore you.

PHILOCTETES

Never, if of my own will I must see Troy.

NEOPTOLEMUS

What shall we do, since I cannot convince you
of anything I say? It is easiest for me°   1395
to leave my argument, and for you to live,
as you are living, with no hope of cure.

PHILOCTETES

Let me suffer what I must suffer.
But what you promised to me and clasped my hand,
that you'd bring me home, fulfill it for me, boy.
Do not delay, do not speak again of Troy.   1400
I have had enough of such talk.

NEOPTOLEMUS

If you will then, let us go.

PHILOCTETES

                        Noble is the word you spoke.

NEOPTOLEMUS

Brace yourself, stand firm on your feet.

PHILOCTETES

                        To the limit of my strength.

NEOPTOLEMUS

How shall I avoid the blame of the Greeks?

PHILOCTETES

                        Give it no thought.

NEOPTOLEMUS

What if they come and harry my country?

PHILOCTETES

                        I shall be there.   1405

NEOPTOLEMUS

What help will you be able to give me?

PHILOCTETES

    With the bow of Heracles.

NEOPTOLEMUS

  Will you?

PHILOCTETES

    I shall drive them from your country.°

NEOPTOLEMUS

  If you will do what you say,

  come now; kiss this ground farewell, and come with me.

      (Heracles appears on high, above the cave of Philoctetes.)°

HERACLES [*chanting*]

  Not yet, not until you have heard

  my words, son of Poias.

  I am the voice of Heracles in your ears;   1410

  I am the shape of Heracles before you.

  It is for your sake I come and leave my home in the heavens.

  I come to tell you of the plans of Zeus,   1415

  to turn you back from the road you go upon.

  Hearken to my words.

  [*now speaking*]

  Let me reveal to you my own story first,

  let me tell you the labors and sufferings that were mine,

  and, at the last, the winning of deathless merit.   1420

  All this you can see in me now,

  all this must be your experience too:

  out of this suffering to win a glorious life,

    Go with this man to the city of Troy.

  First, you shall find there the cure of your cruel sickness,

  and then be adjudged best warrior among the Greeks.   1425

  Paris, the cause of all this evil, you shall kill

  with the bow that was mine. Troy you shall take.

  You shall win the prize of valor from the army

  and shall bring the spoils to your home,

to your father Poias, and the land of your fathers, Oeta.   1430
From the spoils of the campaign you must dedicate
some, on my pyre, in memory of my bow.

Son of Achilles, I have the same words for you.
You shall not have the strength to capture Troy
without this man, nor he without you,   1435
but, like twin lions hunting together,
he shall guard you, you him. I shall send Asclepius
to Ilium to heal his sickness. A second time
must Ilium fall to my bow. But remember this,   1440
when you come to sack that town, revere the gods.
All else our father Zeus thinks of less importance.
Holiness does not die with the men that die.
Whether they die or live, it cannot perish.

PHILOCTETES [*chanting, with Heracles and the Chorus chanting in
response, to the end of the play*]
Voice that stirs my yearning when I hear,   1445
my friend lost for so long,
I shall not disobey.

NEOPTOLEMUS
Nor I.

HERACLES
Do not tarry then.
The moment and the tide are hastening you on your way.   1450

PHILOCTETES
Lemnos, I call upon you:
Farewell, cave that shared my watches,
nymphs of the meadow and the stream,
the deep male growl of the sea-lashed headland   1455
where often, in my niche within the rock,
my head was wet with fine spray,
where many a time in answer to my crying
in the storm of my sorrow the mountain of Hermes sent its echo! 1460

Now springs and Lycian well, I am leaving you,
leaving you.
I had never hoped for this.
Farewell Lemnos, sea-encircled,
blame me not but send me on my way   1465
with a fair voyage to where a great destiny
awaits me, and the judgment of friends and the all-conquering
divinity who has brought this to pass.

CHORUS
    Let us go all
    when we have prayed to the nymphs of the sea   1470
    to bring us safe to our homes.

                            (Exit all.)

OEDIPUS AT COLONUS

SOPHOCLES
Translated by Robert Fitzgerald

INTRODUCTION TO SOPHOCLES' OEDIPUS AT COLONUS

This play is to be dated about 408 or 407 BCE: Sophocles was almost ninety years old when he wrote it, and it was first produced after his death, by his son. The legendary action of the play would fall between the end of *Oedipus the King* and the beginning of *Antigone*, but in a sense it is a sequel to both, for Sophocles seems to have drawn on his own characterization of Oedipus in the former and of Antigone, Ismene, and, in part, Creon in the latter.

The myth follows one variant of Oedipus' end, according to which, after being outcast from all other countries and his own, he was at last received by Theseus, king of Athens, at Sophocles' own birthplace, Colonus, in the territory of Attica. After an oracle had announced that Oedipus' spirit after his death would bring special protection to the land that harbored his corpse, Creon pursued him there, tried to drag him away, and kidnapped his faithful daughters; Theseus intervened and rescued the girls. Then Polynices, Oedipus' estranged son, arrived to ask his blessing and help, but received only curses. Finally Oedipus miraculously passed from this world, to be established in the holy ground as a guardian of Athens for centuries to come.

OEDIPUS AT COLONUS

*Scene: A grove in Colonus dedicated to the Furies. A statue or stele
of the legendary horseman-hero Colonus can be seen on one side.
There is a flat rock, sacred throne of the Furies, in the middle of the
orchestra, and another low outcrop of rock to one side.*

(*Enter Oedipus from one side, old, blind, and ragged, led by Antigone.*)

OEDIPUS
    My daughter—daughter of the blind old man—
    where have we come to now, Antigone?
    What lands are these, or holdings of what city?
    Who will be kind to Oedipus this evening°
    and give alms to the wanderer?
    Though he ask little and receive still less,   5
    it is sufficient:
                    suffering and time,
    vast time, have been instructors in contentment,
    which kingliness° teaches too.

But now, child,
if you can see a resting place—perhaps
a roadside fountain, or some holy grove,   10
tell me and let me pause there and sit down:
so we may learn our whereabouts, and take
our cue from what we hear, as strangers should.

ANTIGONE

Father, poor tired Oedipus, the towers
that crown the city still seem far away;   15
as for this place, it is clearly a holy one,
shady with vines and olive trees and laurel;
a covert for the song and hush of nightingales
in their snug wings.
                    But rest on this rough stone.
It was a long road for an old man to travel.   20

OEDIPUS

Help me sit down; take care of the blind man.

ANTIGONE

After so long, you need not tell me, father.

                    (Antigone helps Oedipus sit down on the rock, at center.)

OEDIPUS

What can you say, now, as to where we are?

ANTIGONE

This place I do not know; I know the city
must be Athens.

OEDIPUS

                    As all the travelers said.   25

ANTIGONE

Then shall I go and ask what place this is?

OEDIPUS

Do, child, if there is any life nearby.

ANTIGONE

Oh, but indeed there is; I need not leave you;
I see a man, now, not far away from us.

OEDIPUS

Is he coming this way? Has he started toward us?   30

(Enter a Stranger, from the side.)

ANTIGONE

Here he is now.
                    Say what seems best to you,
father; the man is here.

OEDIPUS

Friend, my daughter's eyes serve for my own.
She tells me we are fortunate enough to meet you;
and no doubt you will inform us—   35

STRANGER

                    Do not go on!
First, move from where you sit; the place is holy;
it is forbidden to walk upon that ground.

OEDIPUS

What ground is this? What god is honored here?

STRANGER

It is not to be touched, no one may live upon it;
most dreadful are its divinities, most feared,
Daughters of Darkness and mysterious Earth.   40

OEDIPUS

Under what solemn name shall I invoke them?

STRANGER

The people here prefer to address them as Gentle
All-Seeing Ones; elsewhere there are other names.

OEDIPUS

Then may they be gentle to the suppliant;
for I shall never leave this resting place.   45

STRANGER

What is the meaning of this?

OEDIPUS

It was ordained;
I recognize it now.

STRANGER

Without authority
from the city government I dare not move you;
first I must show them what you are doing.

OEDIPUS

Friend, in the name of god, bear with me now!
I turn to you for light; answer the wanderer.°   50

STRANGER

Speak. You will have no discourtesy from me.

OEDIPUS

What is this region that we two have entered?

STRANGER

As much as I can tell you, I will tell.
This country, all of it, is blessed ground;
the god Poseidon loves it; in it the fire carrier
Prometheus has his influence; in particular   55
that spot you rest on has been called this earth's
Doorsill of Brass, and buttress of great Athens.
All men of this land claim descent from him
who is sculptured here, Colonus master horseman,
and bear his name in common with their own.   60
That is this country, stranger: honored less
in histories than in the hearts of the people.

OEDIPUS

Then people live here on their lands?

STRANGER

They do,
the clan of those descended from that hero.   65

OEDIPUS

Ruled by a prince? Or by the greater number?

STRANGER

The land is governed from Athens, by the king.

OEDIPUS

And who is he whose word has power here?

STRANGER

Theseus, son of Aegeus, the king before him.

OEDIPUS

Ah. Would someone then go to this king for me?   70

STRANGER

To tell him what? Perhaps to urge his coming?

OEDIPUS

To tell him a small favor will gain him much.

STRANGER

What service can a blind man render him?

OEDIPUS

All I shall say will be clear-sighted indeed.

STRANGER

Friend, listen to me: I wish you no injury;   75
you seem wellborn, though obviously unlucky;
stay where you are, exactly where I found you.
And I'll inform the people of what you say—
not in the town, but here—it rests with them
to decide if you should stay or must move on.   80

(Exit Stranger, to the side.)

OEDIPUS

Child, has he gone?

ANTIGONE

Yes, father. Now you may speak tranquilly,
for only I am with you.

OEDIPUS   *(Praying.)*
                        Ladies whose eyes
are terrible, Spirits, upon your sacred ground
I have first bent my knees in this new land;   85
therefore be mindful of me and of Apollo.
For when he gave me oracles of evil,
he also spoke of this: a resting place,
after long years, in the last country, where
I should find home among the sacred Furies: 90
that I might round out there my bitter life,
conferring benefit on those who received me,
a curse on those who have driven me away.
Portents, he said, would make me sure of this:
earthquake, thunder, or god's smiling lightning.°   95
But I am sure of it now, sure that you guided me
with feathery certainty° upon this road,
and led me here into your hallowed wood.
How otherwise could I, in my wandering,
have sat down first with you in all this land,
I who drink not, with you who love not wine?   100
How otherwise had I found this chair of stone?
Grant me then, goddesses, passage from life at last,
and consummation, as the unearthly voice foretold;°
unless indeed I seem not worth your grace,
slave as I am to such unending pain   105
as no man had before.
O hear my prayer,
sweet children of original Darkness! Hear me,
Athens, city named for great Athena,
honored above all cities in the world!
Pity a man's poor carcass and his ghost,
for Oedipus is not the strength he was.   110

ANTIGONE
Be still. Some old, old men are coming this way,
looking for the place where you are seated.

OEDIPUS

I shall be still. You get me clear of the path
and hide me in the wood, so I may hear
what they are saying. If we know their temper,   115
we shall be better able to act with prudence.

<blockquote>(Oedipus and Antigone move to one side, into the
grove. Enter the Chorus, from the other side.)</blockquote>

CHORUS [singing]

STROPHE A

Look for him. Who could he be? Where
is he? Where is the stranger
impious, blasphemous, shameless?   120
Use your eyes, search him out!
Cover the ground and uncover him!
Vagabond!
The old man must be a vagabond,
not of our land, for he'd never   125
otherwise dare to go in there,
in the inviolate thicket
of those whom it's futile to fight,°
those whom we tremble to name.
When we pass we avert our eyes—   130
            close our eyes!—
in silence, without conversation,
shaping our prayers with our lips.
But now, if the story is credible,
some alien fool has profaned it.
Yet I have looked over all the grove and   135
still cannot see him,
cannot say where he has hidden.

<blockquote>(Oedipus comes forward with Antigone.)</blockquote>

OEDIPUS [chanting in turn with the Chorus]

That stranger is I. As they say of the blind:
sounds are the things I see.

CHORUS

Ah!

His face is dreadful! His voice is dreadful!   140

OEDIPUS

I beg you not to think of me as a criminal.

CHORUS

Zeus defend us, who is this old man?

OEDIPUS

One whose fate is not quite to be envied.   145
O my masters, and men of this land;
that must be evident: why, otherwise,
should I need this girl
to lead me, her frailty to put my weight on?

CHORUS [*now singing*]

ANTISTROPHE A

Ah! His eyes are blind!   150
And were you brought into the world so?
Unhappy life—and so long!
Well, not if I can stop it
will you have this curse as well.
            Stranger! You
trespass there! But beyond there,   155
in the glade where the grass is still,
where the honeyed libations drip
in the rill from the brimming spring,
you must not step. O stranger,   160
it is well to be careful about it!
Most careful!
Stand aside and come down then!
There is too much space between us!°
Say, wanderer, can you hear?   165
If you have a mind to tell us
your business, or wish to converse with our council,

come away from that place!
Only speak where it's proper to do so!

OEDIPUS [*chanting in turn with Antigone*]
Now, daughter, what is the way of wisdom?   170

ANTIGONE
We must do just as they do here, father;°
we should give in now, and listen to them.

OEDIPUS
Stretch out your hand to me.

ANTIGONE
            There, I am with you.

OEDIPUS
Sirs, let there be no injustice done me,
once I have trusted you, and left my refuge.   175

                    (Led by Antigone, he moves forward.)

CHORUS [*singing in turn with Antigone and Oedipus*]
                    STROPHE B
Never, never, will anyone drive you away
from rest in this land, old man!

OEDIPUS
Shall I come farther?

CHORUS
            Yes, farther.

OEDIPUS
And now?   180

CHORUS
            You must guide him, girl;
you can see how much further to come.

ANTIGONE

Come with your blind step, father;
this way; come where I lead you.

. . . .

CHORUS°

Stranger in a strange country,
courage, afflicted man!   185
Whatever the state abhors,
you too abhor, and honor
whatever the state holds dear.

OEDIPUS [chanting]

Lead me on, then, child,
to where we may speak or listen respectfully.   190
Let us not fight necessity.

CHORUS [singing]

ANTISTROPHE B

Now! Go no further than that platform there,
formed of the natural rock.

OEDIPUS

This?   195

CHORUS

Far enough; you can hear us.

OEDIPUS

Shall I sit down?

CHORUS

Yes, sit there to the side,
at the edge of the rock.

ANTIGONE

Father, this is where I can help you;
you must keep step with me; gently now.

OEDIPUS

Ah, me!

ANTIGONE

    Lean your old body on my arm;   200

    it is I, who love you; let yourself down.

OEDIPUS

    How bitter blindness is!

                             (He is seated on the rock, center.)

CHORUS

    Now that you are at rest, poor man,

    tell us, what is your name?

    Who are you, wanderer?   205

    What is the land of your ancestors?

OEDIPUS [*singing in turn with Antigone and the Chorus*]

                   EPODE

    I am an exile, friends; but do not ask me ...

CHORUS

    What is it you fear to say, old man?

OEDIPUS

    No, no, no! Do not go on

    questioning me! Do not ask my name!   210

CHORUS

    Why not?

OEDIPUS

                My star was unspeakable.°

CHORUS

                      Speak!

OEDIPUS

    My child, what can I say to them?

CHORUS

    Answer us, stranger: what is your family?   215

    Who was your father?

OEDIPUS

God help me, what will become of me, child?

ANTIGONE

Tell them; there is no other way.

OEDIPUS

Well, then, I will; I cannot hide it.

CHORUS

Between you, you greatly delay. Speak up!   220

OEDIPUS

Have you heard of Laius' family?

CHORUS

                              Ah!

OEDIPUS

Of the race of Labdacidae?

CHORUS

                         Ah, Zeus!

OEDIPUS

And ruined Oedipus?

CHORUS

                         You are he!

OEDIPUS

Do not take fright from what I say—

CHORUS

Oh, dreadful!

OEDIPUS

                         I am accursed.

CHORUS

                         Oh, fearful!

OEDIPUS

Antigone, what will happen now?   225

CHORUS

Away with you! Out with you! Leave our country!

OEDIPUS

> And what of the promises you made me?

CHORUS

> God will not punish the man
> who makes return for an injury. 230
> Deceivers may be deceived:
> they play a game that ends
> in grief, and not in pleasure.
> Leave this grove at once!
> Our country is not for you! 235
> Wind no further
> your clinging evil upon us!°

ANTIGONE [still singing]

> O men of reverent mind!
> Since you will not suffer my father,
> old man though he is
> and though you know his story—
> he never knew what he did— 240
> take pity still on my unhappiness;
> and let me intercede with you for him.
> Not with lost eyes, but looking in your eyes
> as if I were a child of yours, I beg 245
> mercy for him, the beaten man! O hear me!
> We are thrown upon your mercy as on god's;
> be kinder than you seem!°
> By all you have and own that is dear to you,
> children, wives, possessions, gods, I pray you! 250
> For you will never see in all the world
> a man whom god has led
> escape his destiny!°

CHORUS LEADER [now speaking]

> Child of Oedipus, indeed we pity you,
> just as we pity him for his misfortune. 255
> But we tremble to think of what the gods may do;
> we dare not speak more generously!

OEDIPUS [*speaking*]

What use is reputation then? What good
comes of a noble name? A noble fiction!
For Athens, so they say, excels in piety;   260
has power to save the wretched of other lands,
can give them refuge, is unique in this.
Yet, when it comes to me, where is her refuge?
You pluck me from these rocks and cast me out,
all for fear of a name!   265
             Or do you dread
my strength? my actions? I think not, for I
suffered those deeds more than I acted them,
as I might show if it were fitting here
to tell my father's and my mother's story . . .
for which you fear me, as I know too well.
And yet, how was I evil in myself?   270
I had been wronged, I retaliated; even had I
known what I was doing, was that evil?
Then, knowing nothing, I went on. Went on.
But those who wronged me knew, and ruined me.
Therefore I beg of you before the gods,   275
for the same cause that made you move me—
in reverence of your gods—give me this shelter,
and thus accord those powers what is theirs.
Think: their eyes are fixed upon the just,
fixed on the unjust too;° no impious man   280
can twist away from them forever.
Now, in their presence, do not blot your city's
luster by bending to unholy action.
As you would receive an honest petitioner,
give me, too, sanctuary; though my face   285
be dreadful in its look, yet honor me!
For I come here as one endowed with grace
by those who are over Nature; and I bring
advantage to this race, as you may learn

more fully when some lord of yours is here.°   290
Meanwhile be careful to be just.

CHORUS LEADER
                    Old man.
This argument of yours compels our wonder.
It was not feebly worded. I am content
that higher authorities should judge this matter.   295

OEDIPUS
And where is he who rules the land, strangers?

CHORUS LEADER
In his father's city; but the messenger
who sent us here has gone to fetch him also.

OEDIPUS
Do you think a blind man will so interest him
as to bring him such a distance?   300

CHORUS LEADER
I do, indeed, when he has heard your name.

OEDIPUS
But who will tell him that?

CHORUS LEADER
It is a long road, and the rumors of travelers
have a way of wandering. He will have word of them.
Take heart—he will be here. Old man, your name   305
has gone over all the earth; though he may be
at rest when the news comes, he will come quickly.

OEDIPUS
Then may he come with luck for his own city
as well as for me. . . . The good befriend themselves.

ANTIGONE
O Zeus! What shall I say? How interpret this?   310

OEDIPUS
Antigone, my dear child, what is it?

ANTIGONE

> A woman
riding a Sicilian pony and coming toward us;
she is wearing the wide Thessalian sun hat.
I don't know! 315
Is it or isn't it? Or am I dreaming?
I think so; yes!—no. I can't be sure . . .
Ah, poor child,
it is no one else but she! And she is smiling 320
now as she comes! It is my dear Ismene!

OEDIPUS

What did you say, child?

(Ismene enters, with one attendant, from the side.)

ANTIGONE

> That I see your daughter!
My sister! Now you can tell her by her voice.

ISMENE

O father and sister together, dearest voices!° 325
Now I have found you—how, I scarcely know—
I don't know how I shall see you through my tears!

OEDIPUS

Child, have you come?

ISMENE

> Father, how old you seem!°

OEDIPUS

Child, are you here?

ISMENE

> And such a time I had!

OEDIPUS

Touch me, little one.

ISMENE

       I shall hold you both!

OEDIPUS

My children . . . and sisters.

ISMENE

       Oh, unhappy people!   330

OEDIPUS

She and I?

ISMENE

       And I with you, unhappy.

OEDIPUS

Why have you come, child?

ISMENE

       Thinking of you, father.

OEDIPUS

You were lonely?

ISMENE

       Yes; and I bring news for you.
I came with the one person I could trust.

OEDIPUS

Why, where are your brothers? Could they not do it?   335

ISMENE

They are—where they are. It is a hard time for them.

OEDIPUS

Ah! They behave as if they were Egyptians,
bred the Egyptian way! Down there, the men
sit indoors all day long, weaving;   340
the women go out and attend to business.
Just so your brothers, who should have done this work,
sit by the fire like home-loving girls,

and you two, in their place, must bear my hardships.   345
One, since her childhood ended and her body
gained its strength, has wandered ever with me,
an old man's governess; often in the wild
forest going without shoes, and hungry,
beaten by many rains, tired by the sun;   350
yet she rejected the sweet life of home
so that her father should have sustenance.
And you, my daughter, once before came out
unknown to Thebes, bringing me news of all
the oracle had said concerning me;   355
and you remained my faithful outpost there,
when I was driven from that land.
               But now,
what news, Ismene, do you bring your father?
Why have you left your house to make this journey?
You came for no light reason, I know that;
it must be something serious for me.   360

ISMENE
I will pass over the troubles I have had
searching for your whereabouts, father.
They were hard enough to bear; and I will not
go through it all again in telling of them.
In any case, it is your sons' troubles   365
that I have come to tell you.
First it was their desire, as it was Creon's,
that the throne should pass to him; that thus the city
should be defiled no longer: such was their reasoning
when they considered our people's ancient curse
and how it enthralled your pitiful family.   370
But then some fury put it in their hearts—°
O pitiful again!—to itch for power,
for seizure of prerogative and throne.
And it was the younger and the less mature
who stripped his elder brother, Polynices,   375

of place and kingship, and then banished him.
But now the people hear he has gone to Argos,
into the valley land, has joined that nation,°
and is enlisting friends among its warriors:
telling them Argos shall honorably win   380
Thebes and her plain, or else eternal glory.°
This is not a mere recital, father,
but terrible truth!
How long will it be, I wonder,
before the gods take pity on your distress?

OEDIPUS
You have some hope then that they are concerned
with my deliverance?

ISMENE
                    I have, father.   385
The latest sentences of the oracle.

OEDIPUS
How are they worded? What do they prophesy?

ISMENE
That you shall be much solicited by our people
before your death—and after—for their welfare.   390

OEDIPUS
And what could anyone hope from such as I?

ISMENE
The oracles declare their strength's in you.

OEDIPUS
When I am worn to nothing, strength in me?

ISMENE
For the gods who threw you down sustain you now.

OEDIPUS
Slight favor, now I am old! My doom was early.   395

ISMENE

The proof of it is that Creon is coming to you
for that same reason, and soon: not by and by.

OEDIPUS

To do what, daughter? Tell me about this.

ISMENE

To settle you near the land of Thebes, and so
have you at hand; but you may not cross the border.   400

OEDIPUS

What good am I to Thebes outside the country?

ISMENE

It is merely that if your burial were unlucky
that would be perilous for them.

OEDIPUS

                    Ah, then!
This does not need divine interpretation.

ISMENE

Therefore they want to keep you somewhere near,
just at the border, where you'll not be free.   405

OEDIPUS

And will they compose my shade with Theban dust?°

ISMENE

Ah, father! No. Your father's blood forbids it.

OEDIPUS

Then they shall never hold me in their power!

ISMENE

If not, some day it will be bitter for them.

OEDIPUS

How will that be, my child?   410

ISMENE

       When they shall stand
where you are buried, and feel your anger there.

OEDIPUS

What you have said—from whom did you hear it, child?

ISMENE

The envoys told me when they returned from Delphi.

OEDIPUS

Then all this about me was spoken there?

ISMENE

According to those men, just come to Thebes.   415

OEDIPUS

Has either of my sons had word of this?

ISMENE

They both have, and they understand it well.

OEDIPUS

The scoundrels! So they knew all this, and yet
would not give up the throne to have me back?

ISMENE

It hurts me to hear it, but I can't deny it.   420

OEDIPUS

Gods!
Never quench their fires of ambition!
Let the last word be mine upon this battle
they are about to join, with the spears lifting!
I'd see that he who holds the scepter now   425
will not have power long, nor would the other,
the banished one, return!
         These were the two
who saw me in disgrace and banishment

and never lifted a hand for me. They heard me
howled from the country, heard the thing proclaimed!   430
And would you say I wanted exile then,
an appropriate clemency, granted by the state?
That is all false! The truth is that at first
my mind was a boiling caldron; nothing so sweet
as death, death by stoning, could have been given me;   435
yet no one there would grant me that desire.
It was only later, when my madness cooled,
and I had begun to think my rage excessive,
my punishment too great for what I had done;
then it was that the city—in its good time!—   440
decided to be harsh, and drove me out.
They could have helped me then; they could have
helped him who begot them! Would they do it?
For lack of a little word from that fine pair
out I went, a beggar, to wander forever!
Only by grace of these two girls, unaided,   445
have I got food or shelter or devotion;
their two brothers held their father of less worth
than sitting on a throne and being king.
Well, they shall never win me in their fight,°   450
nor will they profit from the rule of Thebes.
I am sure of that; I have heard the prophecies
brought by this girl; I think they fit those others
spoken so long ago, and now fulfilled.

So let Creon be sent to find me: Creon,   455
or any other of influence in the state.
If you men here consent—as do those powers
holy and awful, the Spirits of this place—
to give me refuge, then shall this city have
a great savior, and woe to my enemies!   460

CHORUS LEADER
Oedipus: you are surely worth our pity:
you, and your children, too. And since you claim

also to be a savior of our land,
I'd like to give you counsel for good luck.

CHORUS LEADER

Dear friend! I'll do whatever you advise.   465

CHORUS LEADER

Make expiation to these divinities
whose ground you violated when you came.

OEDIPUS

In what way shall I do so? Tell me, friends.

CHORUS LEADER

First you must bring libations from the spring
that runs forever; and bring them with clean hands.   470

OEDIPUS

And when I have that holy water, then?

CHORUS LEADER

There are some bowls there, by a skillful potter;
put chaplets round the brims, over the handles.

OEDIPUS

Of myrtle sprigs, or woolen stuff, or what?

CHORUS LEADER

Take the fleeces cropped from a young lamb.   475

OEDIPUS

Just so; then how must I perform the rite?

CHORUS LEADER

Facing the quarter of the morning light
pour your libations out.

OEDIPUS

Am I to pour them from the bowls you speak of?

CHORUS LEADER

In three streams, yes; the last one, empty it.

OEDIPUS

With what should it be filled? Tell me this, too.   480

CHORUS LEADER

With water and honey; but with no wine added.

OEDIPUS

And when the leaf-dark earth receives it?

CHORUS LEADER

Lay three times nine young shoots of olive on it
with both your hands; meanwhile repeat this prayer:

OEDIPUS

This—I am eager to hear this, for it has great power.   485

CHORUS LEADER

That as we call them Eumenides,
which means the gentle of heart,
may they accept with gentleness
the suppliant and his wish.
So you, or he who prays for you, address them;
but do not speak aloud or raise a cry;
then come away, and do not turn again.   490
If you will do all this, I shall take heart
and stand up for you; otherwise, O stranger,
I should be seriously afraid for you.

OEDIPUS

Children, you hear the words of these good people?

ANTIGONE

Yes; now tell us what we ought to do.

OEDIPUS

It need not be performed by me; I'm far   495
from having the strength or sight for it—I have neither.
Let one of you go and carry out the ritual.
One soul, I think, often can make atonement
for many others, if it be devoted.

Now do it quickly—yet do not leave me alone!   500
I could not move without the help of someone.

ISMENE

I'll go and do it. But where am I to go?
Where shall I find the holy place, I wonder?

CHORUS LEADER

On the other side of the wood, girl. If you need it,
you may get help from the attendant there.

ISMENE

I am going now. Antigone, you will stay
and care for father. If it were difficult,
I should not think it so, since it is for him.°

(Exit Ismene to the side.)

CHORUS [*singing in turn with Oedipus*]
                      STROPHE A
What evil things have slept since long ago   510
it is not sweet to waken;
and yet I long to be told—

OEDIPUS
                What?

CHORUS
Of that heartbreak for which there was no help,
the pain you have had to suffer.

OEDIPUS
For kindness' sake, do not open   515
my old wound, and my shame.

CHORUS
It is told everywhere, and never dies;
I only want to hear it truly told.

OEDIPUS
Ah! Ah!

CHORUS

Consent I beg you!
Give me my wish, and I shall give you yours.   520

OEDIPUS

ANTISTROPHE A

I had to face a thing most terrible,
not willed by me, I swear;
I would have abhorred it all.

CHORUS

So?

OEDIPUS

Though I did not know, Thebes married me to evil;   525
Fate and I were joined there.

CHORUS

Then it was indeed your mother,
with whom the thing was done?°

OEDIPUS

Ah! It is worse than death to have to hear it!
Strangers! Yes: and these two girls of mine . . .   530

CHORUS

You say—

OEDIPUS

These luckless two
were given birth by her who gave birth to me.

CHORUS

STROPHE B

These then are daughters; they are also—

OEDIPUS

Sisters: yes, their father's sisters . . .   535

CHORUS

Ah, pity!

OEDIPUS

        Pity, indeed. What throngs
of pities come into my mind!

CHORUS

  You suffered—

OEDIPUS

        Yes, unspeakably.

CHORUS

  You sinned—

OEDIPUS

        No, I did not sin!

CHORUS

        How not?

OEDIPUS

        I thought
of her as my reward. Ah, would that I had never won it!   540
Would that I had never served the state that day!°

CHORUS

           ANTISTROPHE B
Unhappy man—and you also killed—

OEDIPUS

What is it now? What are you after?

CHORUS

Killed your father!

OEDIPUS

        God in heaven!
You strike again where I am hurt.

CHORUS

You killed him.   545

OEDIPUS

        Killed him. Yet, there is—

CHORUS
What more?

OEDIPUS
A *just extenuation.*
This:
I did not know him; and he wished to murder me.
Before the law—before god—I am innocent!°

(Enter Theseus from the side, with a retinue of soldiers.)

CHORUS LEADER
The king is coming! Aegeus' eldest son,
Theseus: news of you has brought him here.   550

THESEUS
In the old time I often heard men tell
of the bloody extinction of your eyes.
Even if on my way I were not informed,
I'd recognize you, son of Laius.
The garments and the tortured face   555
make plain your identity. I am sorry for you,
and I should like to know what favor here
you hope for from the city and from me:
both you and your unfortunate companion.
Tell me. It would be something dire indeed   560
to make me leave you comfortless; for I
too was an exile. I grew up abroad;
and in strange lands I fought as few men have
with danger and with death.
Therefore no wanderer shall come, as you do,   565
and be denied my audience or aid.
I know I am only a man; I have no more
to hope for in the end than you have.

OEDIPUS
Theseus, in those few words your nobility
is plain to me. I need not speak at length.   570

You have named me and my father accurately,
spoken with knowledge of my land and exile.
There is, then, nothing left for me to tell
but my desire; and then the tale is ended.

THESEUS
Tell me your wish, then; let me hear it now.   575

OEDIPUS
I come to give you something, and the gift
is my own beaten self: no feast for the eyes;
yet in me is a more lasting grace than beauty.

THESEUS
What grace is this you say you bring to us?°

OEDIPUS
In time you'll learn, but not immediately.   580

THESEUS
How long, then, must we wait to be enlightened?

OEDIPUS
Until I am dead, and you have buried me.

THESEUS
Your wish is burial? What of your life meanwhile?
Have you forgotten that?—or do you care?

OEDIPUS
It is all implicated in my burial.   585

THESEUS
But this is a brief favor you ask of me.

OEDIPUS
See to it, nevertheless! It is not simple.°

THESEUS
You mean I shall have trouble with your sons?

OEDIPUS

Those people want to take me back there now.

THESEUS

Will you not go? Is exile admirable?°   590

OEDIPUS

No. When I wished to go, they would not have it.

THESEUS

What childishness! You are surely in no position—

OEDIPUS

When you know me, admonish me; not now!

THESEUS

Instruct me then. I must not speak in ignorance.

OEDIPUS

Theseus, I have been wounded more than once.   595

THESEUS

Is it your family's curse that you refer to?

OEDIPUS

Not merely that; all Hellas talks of that.

THESEUS

Then what is the wound that is so pitiless?

OEDIPUS

Think how it is with me. I was expelled
from my own land by my own sons; and now,   600
as a parricide, my return is not allowed.

THESEUS

How can they summon you, if this is so?

OEDIPUS

The sacred oracle compels them to.

THESEUS

They fear some punishment from his forebodings?

OEDIPUS

They fear they will be struck down in this land!   605

THESEUS

And how could war arise between these nations?°

OEDIPUS

Most gentle son of Aegeus! The immortal
gods alone have neither age nor death!
All other things almighty Time disquiets.   610
Earth wastes away; the body wastes away;
faith dies; distrust is born;
and imperceptibly the spirit changes
between a man and his friend, or between two cities.
For some men soon, for others in later time,
their pleasure sickens; or love comes again.   615
And so with you and Thebes: the sweet season
holds between you now; but time goes on,
unmeasured Time, fathering numberless
nights, unnumbered days: and on one day
they'll break apart with spears this harmony—
all for a trivial word.   620
And then my sleeping and long-hidden corpse,
cold in the earth, will drink hot blood of theirs,
if Zeus endures; if his son's word is true.

    However: there's no felicity in speaking
of hidden things. Let me come back to this: 625
be careful that you keep your word to me;
for if you do you'll never say of Oedipus
that he was given refuge uselessly—
or if you say it, then the gods have lied.

CHORUS LEADER

My lord: before you came this man gave promise
of having power to make his words come true.   630

THESEUS

Who would reject his friendship? Is he not

one who would have, in any case, an ally's
right to our hospitality?
Moreover he has asked grace of our deities,
and offers no small favor in return.   635
As I value that favor, I shall not refuse
this man's desire; I declare him a citizen.
And if it should please our friend to remain here,
I direct you to take care of him;
or else he may come with me.
                    Whatever you choose,   640
Oedipus, we shall be happy to accord.
You know your own needs best; I accede to them.

OEDIPUS
May god bless men like these!

THESEUS
What do you say then? Shall it be my house?

OEDIPUS
If it were right for me. But the place is here . . .

THESEUS
And what will you do here?—not that I oppose you.   645

OEDIPUS
Here I shall prevail over those who banished me.

THESEUS
Your presence, as you say, is a great blessing.

OEDIPUS
If you are firm in doing what you promise.

THESEUS
You can be sure of me; I'll not betray you.

OEDIPUS
I'll not ask pledges, as I would of scoundrels.   650

THESEUS

You'd get no more assurance than by my word.

OEDIPUS

I wonder how you will behave?

THESEUS

        You fear?

OEDIPUS

That men will come—

THESEUS

        These men will attend to them.

OEDIPUS

Look: when you leave me—

THESEUS

        I know what to do!

OEDIPUS

I am oppressed by fear!

THESEUS

        I feel no fear.   655

OEDIPUS

You do not know the menace!

THESEUS

        I do know
no man is going to take you against my will.
Angry men are liberal with threats°
and bluster generally. When the mind
is master of itself, threats are no matter.   660
These people may have dared to talk quite fiercely
of taking you; perhaps, as I rather think,
they'll find a sea of troubles in the way.
Therefore I should advise you to take heart.

Even aside from me and my intentions,
did not Apollo send and guide you here?   665
However it may be, I can assure you,
while I'm away, my name will be your shield.

(Exit Theseus and soldiers, to the side.)

CHORUS [*singing*]

STROPHE A

The land of running horses, fair
Colonus takes a guest;   670
he shall not seek another home.°
For this, in all the earth and air,
is most secure and loveliest.

In the god's untrodden vale
where leaves and berries throng,
and wine-dark ivy climbs the bough,
the sweet, sojourning nightingale   675
murmurs all night long.

No sun nor wind may enter there
nor the winter's rain;
but ever through the shadow goes
Dionysus reveler,
immortal maenads in his train.   680

ANTISTROPHE A

Here with drops of heaven's dews
at daybreak all the year,
the clusters of narcissus bloom,
time-hallowed garlands for the brows
of those great Ladies whom we fear.

The crocus like a little sun
blooms with its yellow ray;   685
the river's fountains are awake,
and his nomadic streams that run
unthinned forever, and never stay,°

But like perpetual lovers move
on the maternal land.   690
And here the choiring Muses come,
and the divinity of Love,
with the gold reins in her hand.

And our land has a thing unknown
on Asia's sounding coast   695
or in the sea-surrounded west
where Pelops' kin holds sway:°
the olive, fertile and self-sown,
the terror of our enemies
that no hand tames nor tears away—
the blessed tree that never dies!—   700
but it will mock the spearsman in his rage.

Ah, how it flourishes in every field,
most beautifully here!
The gray-leafed tree, the children's nourisher!
No young man nor one partnered by his age
knows how to root it out nor make
barren its yield;
for Zeus Protector of the Shoot has sage   705
eyes that forever are awake,
and Pallas watches with her sea-gray eyes.

Last and grandest praise I sing
to Athens, nurse of men,
for her great pride and for the splendor   710
destiny has conferred on her.
Land from which fine horses spring!
Land where foals are beautiful!
Land of the sea and the seafarer,
enthroned on her pure littoral
by Cronus' briny son in ancient time.

That lord, Poseidon, must I praise again
who found our horsemen fit   715
for first bestowal of the curb and bit,
to discipline the stallion in his prime;
and strokes to which our oarsmen sing,
well-fitted, oak and men,
whose long sea-oars in wondrous rhyme
flash from the salt foam, following
the track of winds on waters virginal.°

ANTIGONE

Land so well spoken of and praised so much!   720
Now is the time to show those words are true.

OEDIPUS

What now, my child?

ANTIGONE

                    A man is coming toward us,
and it is Creon—not alone, though, father.

OEDIPUS

Most kindly friends! I hope you may give proof,
and soon, of your ability to protect me!   725

CHORUS LEADER

No fear: it will be proved. I may be old,
but the nation's strength has not grown old.

                              (*Enter Creon from the side, with soldiers.*)

CREON

Gentlemen, and citizens of this land:
I can see from your eyes that my arrival
has been a cause of sudden fear to you.   730
Do not be fearful; and say nothing hostile!
I have not come for any hostile action:
for I am old, and know this city has
power, if any city in Hellas has.

But for this man here: I, despite my age,   735
am sent to bring him to the land of Thebes.°
This is not one man's mission, but was ordered
by the whole Theban people. I am their emissary,
because it fell to me as a relative
to mourn his troubles more than anyone.
        So, now, poor Oedipus, come home.   740
You know the word I bring. Your countrymen
are right in summoning you—I most of all,
for most of all, unless I am worst of men,
I grieve for your unhappiness, old man.
I see you ravaged as you are, a stranger   745
everywhere, never at rest,
with only a girl to serve you in your need—
I never thought she'd fall to such indignity,
poor child! And yet she has,
forever tending you, leading a beggar's   750
life with you; a grown-up girl who knows
nothing of marriage; whoever comes can take her . . .
        Is not this a disgrace? I weep to see it!
Disgrace for you, for me, for all our people!
We cannot hide what is so palpable.   755
But you, if you will listen to me, Oedipus—
and in the name of your father's gods, listen!—
bury the whole thing now;° agree with me
to go back to your city and your home!
Take friendly leave of Athens, as she merits;
but you should have more reverence for Thebes,
since long ago she was your kindly nurse.   760

OEDIPUS

You brazen rascal! Playing your rascal's tricks
in righteous speeches, as you always would!
Why do you try it? How can you think to take me
into that snare I should so hate if taken?
That time when I was sick with my own life's   765

evil, when I would gladly have left my land,
you had no mind to give me what I wanted!
But when at long last I had had my fill
of rage and grief, and in my quiet house
began to find some comfort: that was the time
you chose to rout me out. 770
How precious was this kinship to you then?
It is the same thing now: you see this city
and all its people being kind to me,
so you would draw me away—
a cruel thing, for all your soothing words.
Why is it your pleasure to be amiable 775
to those who do not want your amiability?
Suppose that when you begged for something desperately
a man should neither grant it you nor give
sympathy even; but later when you were glutted
with all your heart's desire, should give it then,
when charity was no charity at all?
Would you not think the kindness somewhat hollow? 780
That is the sort of kindness you offer me:
generous in words, but in reality evil.
Now I will tell these men, and prove you evil.
You come to take me, but not to take me home;
rather to settle me outside the city 785
so that the city may escape my curse,
escape from punishment by Athens.
                    Yes;
but you'll not have it. What you'll have is this:
my vengeance active in that land forever.
And what my sons will have of my old kingdom
is just so much room as they need to die in! 790
    Now who knows better the destiny of Thebes?
I do, for I have had the best informants:
Apollo, and Zeus himself who is his father.
And yet you come here with your fraudulent speech

all whetted up! The more you talk, the more   795
harm, not good, you'll get by it!—
however, I know you'll never believe that—
only leave us! Let us live here in peace!
Is this misfortune, if it brings contentment?

CREON

Which of us do you consider is more injured   800
by talk like this? You hurt only yourself.

OEDIPUS

I am perfectly content, so long as you
can neither wheedle me nor fool these others.

CREON

Unhappy man! Shall it be plain that time
brings you no wisdom? that you shame your age?   805

OEDIPUS

An agile wit! I know no honest man
able to speak so well under all conditions!

CREON

To speak much is one thing; to speak to the point's another!

OEDIPUS

As if you spoke so little but so fittingly!

CREON

No, not fittingly for a mind like yours!   810

OEDIPUS

Leave me! I speak for these men, too!
Spare me your wardship, here where I must live!

CREON

I call on these—not you!—as witnesses
of what rejoinder you have made to friends.
If I ever take you—

OEDIPUS

With these men opposing,
who is going to take me by violence?   815

CREON

You'll suffer without need of that, I promise you!

OEDIPUS

What are you up to? What is behind that brag?

CREON

Your daughters: one of them I have just now
had seized and carried off; now I'll take this one!

OEDIPUS

Ah!

CREON

                    Soon you shall have more reason to groan about it!   820

OEDIPUS

You have my child?

CREON

                    And this one in a moment!

OEDIPUS

Ah, friends! What will you do? Will you betray me?
Expel this man who has profaned your country!

CHORUS LEADER

Go, and go quickly, stranger! You have no right
to do what you are doing, or what you have done!   825

CREON   *(To his soldiers.)*

You there: it would be well to take her now,
whether she wants to go with you or not.

                                        (Two soldiers approach Antigone.)

ANTIGONE

Oh, god, where shall I run? What help is there
From gods or men?

CHORUS LEADER
          What are you doing, stranger?

CREON
I will not touch this man; but she is mine.   830

OEDIPUS
O masters of this land!

CHORUS LEADER
          This is unjust!

CREON
No, just!

CHORUS LEADER
     Why so?

CREON
          I take what belongs to me!

OEDIPUS [now singing]
                    STROPHE
O Athens!

                         (The soldiers seize Antigone.)

CHORUS [mostly singing while Creon, Antigone, and Oedipus speak in response]
What are you doing, stranger? Will you   835
Let her go? Must we have a test of strength?

CREON
Hold off!

CHORUS
Not while you persist in doing this!

CREON
Your city will have war if you hurt me!

OEDIPUS
Did I not foretell this?

CHORUS LEADER
                Take your hands
off the child at once!

CREON
                What you cannot enforce,
do not command!

CHORUS LEADER
Release the child, I say!

CREON
                And I say—march!   840

CHORUS
Help! Here, men of Colonus! Help! Help!
The city, my city, is violated!
Help, ho!

ANTIGONE
They drag me away. How wretched! O friends, friends!

OEDIPUS
Where are you, child?

ANTIGONE
                They have overpowered me!   845

OEDIPUS
Give me your hands, little one!

ANTIGONE
                I cannot do it!

CREON   *(To the soldiers.)*
Will you get on with her?

                (Exit the guards to one side, dragging Antigone.)

OEDIPUS
                God help me now!°

CREON

With these two sticks at any rate you'll never
guide yourself again. But since you wish
to conquer your own people—by whose command,   850
though I am royal, I have performed this act—
go on and conquer! Later, I think, you'll learn
that now as before you have done yourself no good
by gratifying your temper against your friends!
Anger has always been your greatest sin!   855

CHORUS LEADER   (To Creon, approaching him.)
Control yourself, stranger!

CREON

                Don't touch me, I say!

CHORUS LEADER

I'll not release you! Those two girls were stolen!

CREON

By god, I'll have more plunder in a moment
to bring my city! I'll not stop with them!

CHORUS LEADER

Now what are you about?   860

CREON

                I'll take him, too!

CHORUS LEADER

A terrible thing to say!

CREON

                It will be done!

CHORUS LEADER

Not if the ruler of our land can help it!°

OEDIPUS

Voice of shamelessness! Will you touch me?

CREON

    Silence, I say!

OEDIPUS

               No! May the powers here
not make me silent until I say this curse: 865
you scoundrel, who have cruelly taken her
who served my naked eyepits as their eyes!
On you and yours forever may the sun god,
watcher of all the world, confer such days
as I have had, and such an age as mine!   870

CREON

    Do you see this, men of the land of Athens?

OEDIPUS

    They see both me and you; and they see also
that when I am hurt I have only words to avenge it!

CREON

    I'll not stand for it longer! Alone as I am,
and slow with age, I'll try my strength to take him!   875

                        (Creon advances toward Oedipus.)

OEDIPUS

                ANTISTROPHE

    Ah!

CHORUS

    You are a bold man, friend,
    if you think you can do this!

CREON

    I do think so!

CHORUS

    If you could, our city would be finished!   880

CREON

    In a just cause the weak will beat the strong!

OEDIPUS
You hear his talk?

CHORUS LEADER
By Zeus, he shall not do it!°

CREON
Zeus may determine that, but you will not.

CHORUS LEADER
Is this not criminal?

CREON   (Laying hold of Oedipus.)
If so, you'll bear it!

CHORUS [singing]
Ho, everyone! Captains, ho!
Come on the run!   885
They are well on their way by now!

                    (Enter Theseus from the side, with armed men.)

THESEUS
Why do you shout? What is the matter here?
Of what are you afraid?
You have interrupted me as I was sacrificing
to the great sea god, the patron of Colonus.
Tell me, let me know everything;
I do not care to make such haste for nothing.   890

OEDIPUS
O dearest friend—I recognize your voice—
a fearful thing has just been done to me!

THESEUS
What is it? Who is the man who did it? Tell me.

OEDIPUS
This Creon has had my daughters bound and stolen.   895

THESEUS
What's this you say?

OEDIPUS

       Yes; now you know my loss.

THESEUS *(To his men.)*

One of you go on the double
to the altar place and rouse the people there;
make them leave the sacrifice at once
and run full speed, both foot and cavalry
as hard as they can gallop, for the place   900
where the two highways come together.
The girls must not be taken past that point,
or I shall be a laughingstock to this fellow,
as if I were a man to be handled roughly!
Go on, do as I tell you! Quick!

          (Exit a soldier, to the side.)

       This man—
if I should act in anger, as he deserves,   905
I would not let him leave my hands unbloodied;
but he shall be subject to the sort of laws
he has himself imported here.—

          (To Creon.)

You: you shall never leave this land of Attica
until you produce those girls here in my presence;   910
for your behavior is an affront to me,
a shame to your own people and your nation.
You come to a city-state that practices justice,
a state that rules by law, and by law only;
and yet you cast aside her authority,   915
take what you please, and worse, by violence,
as if you thought there were no men among us,
or only slaves; and as if I were nobody.

     I doubt that Thebes is responsible for you:
she has no propensity for breeding rascals.   920
And Thebes would not applaud you if she knew
you tried to trick me and to rob the gods

by dragging helpless people from their sanctuary!
Were I a visitor in your country—
no matter how immaculate my claims—   925
without consent from him who ruled the land,
whoever he might be, I'd take nothing.
I think I have some notion of the conduct
proper to one who visits a friendly city.
You bring disgrace upon an honorable
land—your own land, too; a long life   930
seems to have left you witless as you are old.

    I said it once and say it now again:
someone had better bring those girls here quickly,
unless you wish to prolong your stay with us
under close guard, and not much liking it.   935
This is not just a speech; I mean it, friend.

CHORUS LEADER
Now do you see where you stand? Thebes is just;
but you are adjudged to have acted wickedly.

CREON
It was not that I thought this state unmanly,
son of Aegeus; nor ill-governed, either;   940
rather I did this thing in the opinion
that no one here would love my citizens°
so tenderly as to keep them against my will . . .
And surely, I thought, no one would give welcome
to an unholy man, a parricide,
a man with whom his mother had been found!°   945
Such at least was my estimate of the wisdom
native to the Areopagus; I thought
Athens was not a home for such exiles.
In that belief I considered him my prize.   950
Even so, I'd not have touched him had he not
called down curses on my race and me;
that was an injury that deserved reprisal.
There is no old age for a man's anger.

Only death; the dead cannot be hurt.° 955
　　You will do as you wish in this affair,
for even though my case is right and just,
I am weak, without support. Nevertheless,
old as I am, I'll try to hold you answerable.

OEDIPUS

O arrogance unashamed! Whose age do you 960
think you are insulting, mine or yours?
The bloody deaths, the incest, the calamities
you speak so glibly of: I suffered them
by fate, against my will! It was god's pleasure,
and perhaps our family had angered him long ago.° 965
In me myself you could not find such evil
as would have made me sin against my own.
And tell me this: if there were prophecies
repeated by the oracles of the gods,
that father's death should come through his own son, 970
how could you justly blame it upon me?
On me, who was yet unborn, yet unconceived,
not yet existent for my father and mother?
If then I came into the world—as I did come—
in wretchedness, and met my father in fight
and knocked him down, not knowing that I killed him 975
nor whom I killed°—again, how could you find
guilt in that unmeditated act?
As for my mother—damn you, you have no shame,
though you are her own brother, in forcing me
to speak of that unspeakable marriage;
but I shall speak, I'll not be silent now 980
after you've let your foul talk go so far!
Yes, she gave me birth—incredible fate!—
but neither of us knew the truth; and she
bore my children also—and then her shame.
But one thing I do know: you are content 985
to slander her as well as me for that;

while I would not have married her willingly
nor willingly would I ever speak of it.
No: I shall not be judged an evil man,
neither in that marriage nor in that death
which you forever charge me with so bitterly.   990
     Just answer me one thing:
if someone tried to kill you here and now,
you righteous gentleman, what would you do,
inquire first if the stranger was your father?
Or would you not first try to defend yourself?
I think that since you like to be alive   995
you'd treat him as the threat required; not
look around for assurance that you were right.
Well, that was the sort of danger I was in,
forced into it by the gods. My father's soul,
were it on earth, I know would bear me out.
You, however—being a knave, and since you   1000
think it fair to say anything you choose
and speak of what should not be spoken of—
accuse me of all this before these people.
     You also think it clever to flatter Theseus,
and Athens—her exemplary government.
But in your flattery you have forgotten this: 1005
if any country comprehends the honors
due to the gods, this country knows them best.
Yet you would steal me from Athens in my age
and in my time of prayer;° indeed, you seized me
and you have seized and carried off my daughters.
     Now for that profanation I make my prayer,   1010
calling on the divinities of the grove
that they shall give me aid and fight for me,
so you may know what men defend this town.

CHORUS LEADER
     My lord, our friend is worthy; he has had
     disastrous fortune; yet he deserves our comfort.   1015

THESEUS

Enough of speeches. While the perpetrators
flee, we who were injured loiter here.

CREON

What will you have me do?—since I am worthless.

THESEUS

You lead us on the way. You can be my escort.
If you are holding the children in this neighborhood,   1020
you yourself will uncover them to me.
If your retainers have taken them in flight,
the chase is not ours; others are after them,
and they will never have cause to thank their gods
for getting free out of this country.
All right. Move on. And remember that the captor   1025
is now the captive; the hunter is in the snare.
What was won by stealth will not be kept.
In this you'll not have others to assist you;
and I know well you had them, for you'd never
dare to go so far in your insolence   1030
were you without sufficient accomplices.
You must have had a reason for your confidence,
and I must reckon with it. The whole city
must not seem overpowered by one man.°
Do you understand at all? Or do you think
that what I say is still without importance?   1035

CREON

To what you say I make no objection here.
At home we, too, shall determine what to do.

THESEUS

If you must threaten, do so on the way.
Oedipus, you stay here, and rest assured
that unless I perish first I'll not draw breath   1040
until I put your children in your hands.

OEDIPUS

Bless you for your noble heart, Theseus,
and you are blessed in what you do for us.°

(Exit Theseus and Creon to the side, with the soldiers.)

CHORUS [singing]

STROPHE A

Ah, god, to be where the pillagers make stand!°
To hear the shout and brazen sound of war!   1045
Or maybe on Apollo's sacred strand,
or by that torchlit Eleusinian shore

Where pilgrims come, whose lips the golden key   1050
of sweet-voiced Ministers has rendered still.
To cherish there with grave Persephone
consummate rest from death and mortal ill;

For even to those shades the warrior king   1055
will press the fighting on—until he take
the virgin sisters from the foemen's ring,
within his country, for his country's sake!

ANTISTROPHE A

It may be they will get beyond the plain
and reach the snowy mountain's western side.   1060
If their light chariots have the racing rein,
if they have ponies, and if they can ride;

Yet they'll be taken: for the god they fear
fights for our land, and Theseus sends forth   1065
his breakneck cavalry with all its gear
flashing like mountain lightning to the north.

These are the riders of Athens, conquered never;°
they honor her whose glory all men know,
and honor the sea god, who is dear forever   1070
to Rhea Mother, who bore him long ago.

Swords out—or has the work of swords begun?
My mind leans to a whisper: 1075
within the hour they must surrender
the woeful children of the blinded one;
this day is shaped by Zeus Artificer.
I can call up the bright sword play,°   1080
but wish the wind would lift me like a dove
under the tall cloud cover
to look with my own eyes on this affray.

Zeus, lord of all, and eye of heaven on all,   1085
let our home troop's hard riding
cut them off, and a charge from hiding
carry the combat in one shock and fall.
Stand, helmeted Athena, at our side,   1090
Apollo, Artemis, come down,
hunter and huntress of the flickering deer—
pace with each cavalier
for honor of our land and Athens town.°   1095

CHORUS LEADER [*speaking*]
   O wanderer! You will not say I lied;
   I who kept lookout for you!
   I see them now—the two girls—here they come
   with our armed men around them.

OEDIPUS
   What did you say? Ah, where?

> (*Enter Theseus from the side, leading Antigone*
> *and Ismene, escorted by soldiers.*)

ANTIGONE
                    Father, father!
   I wish some god would give you eyes to see   1100
   the noble prince who brings us back to you!

OEDIPUS

Ah, child! You are really here?

ANTIGONE

Yes, for the might
of Theseus and his kind followers saved us.

OEDIPUS

Come to your father, child, and let me touch you both,
whom I had thought never to touch again!   1105

ANTIGONE

It shall be as you ask; I wish it as much as you.

OEDIPUS

Where are you?

ANTIGONE

We are coming to you together.

OEDIPUS

My sweet children!

ANTIGONE

To our father, sweet indeed.

OEDIPUS

My staff and my support!

ANTIGONE

And partners in sorrow.

OEDIPUS

I have what is dearest to me in the world: 1110
to die, now, would not be so terrible
since you are near me.
              Press close to me, child,
be rooted in your father's arms; rest now
from the cruel separation, the going and coming;
and tell me the story as briefly as you can: 1115
a little talk is enough for girls so tired.°

ANTIGONE

Theseus saved us: he is the one to tell you,
and he can put it briefly and make it clear.°

OEDIPUS

Dear friend: don't be offended if I continue
to talk to these two children overlong;   1120
I had scarce thought they would be seen again!
Be sure I understand that you alone
made this joy possible for me.
You are the one that saved them, no one else,
and may the gods give you such destiny
as I desire for you and for your country.   1125
For I have found you truly reverent,
decent, and straight in speech, you only
of all mankind.
I know it, and I thank you with these words.
All that I have I owe to your courtesy.
Now give me your right hand, my lord,   1130
and if it be permitted, let me kiss you . . .
          What am I saying? How can a wretch like me
desire to touch a man who has no stain
of evil in him? No, no; I will not do it;
and neither shall you touch me. The only ones
fit to be fellow sufferers of mine   1135
are those with such experience as I have.
Receive my salutation where you are;
and for the rest, be kindly to me still
as you have been up to now.

THESEUS

That you should talk a long time to your children
in joy at seeing them—why, that's no wonder!   1140
Or that you should address them before me—
there's no offense in that. It is not in words
that I should wish my life to be distinguished,
but rather in things done.

Have I not shown that? I was not a liar   1145
in what I swore I'd do for you, old man.
I am here; and I have brought them back
alive and safe, for all they were threatened with.
As to how I found them, how I took them, why
brag of it? You will surely learn from them.
However, there is a matter that just now   1150
came to my attention on my way here—
a trivial thing to speak of, and yet puzzling;
I want your opinion on it.
It is best for a man not to neglect such things.

OEDIPUS

What is it, son of Aegeus? Tell me,
so I may know on what you desire counsel.   1155

THESEUS

They say a man is here claiming to be
a relative of yours, though not of Thebes;
for some reason he has thrown himself in prayer°
before Poseidon's altar, where I was making
sacrifice before I came.

OEDIPUS

What is his country? What is he praying for?   1160

THESEUS

All I know is this: he asks, they tell me,
a brief interview with you, and nothing more.

OEDIPUS

Upon what subject?
If he's in prayer, it cannot be a trifle.

THESEUS

They say he only asks to speak to you
and then to depart safely by the same road.   1165

OEDIPUS

Who could it be that would come here to pray?°

THESEUS

Think: have you any relative in Argos
who might desire this favor of you?

OEDIPUS

Dear friend!
Say no more!

THESEUS

What has alarmed you?

OEDIPUS

No more!

THESEUS

But what is the matter? Tell me.   1170

OEDIPUS

When I heard "Argos" I knew the petitioner.

THESEUS

And who is he whom I must hold at fault?

OEDIPUS

A son of mine, my lord, and a hated one:
nothing could be more painful than to listen to him.

THESEUS

But why? Is it not possible to listen   1175
without doing anything you need not do?
Why should it distress you so to hear him?

OEDIPUS

My lord, even his voice is hateful to me.
Don't overrule me; don't make me yield in this!

THESEUS

But now consider if you are not obliged
to do so by his supplication here:
perhaps you have a duty to the god.   1180

ANTIGONE

Father, listen to me, even if I am young.
Allow this man to satisfy his conscience
and give the gods whatever he thinks their due.
And let our brother come here, for our sake.
Don't be afraid: he will not throw you off   1185
in your resolve, nor speak offensively.
What is the harm in hearing what he says?
If he has ill intentions, he'll betray them.
You sired him; even though he wrongs you, father,
and wrongs you impiously, still you cannot   1190
rightfully wrong him in return!
Do let him come!
                    Other men have bad sons,
and other men are swift to anger; yet
they will accept advice, they will be swayed
by their friends' pleading, even against their nature.
Reflect, not on the present, but on the past;   1195
think of your mother's and your father's fate
and what you suffered through them! If you do,
I think you'll see how terrible an end
terrible wrath may have.
You have, I think, a permanent reminder
in your lost, irrecoverable eyes.   1200
Ah, yield to us! If our request is just,
we need not, surely, be importunate;
and you, to whom I have not yet been hard,
should not be obdurate with me!°

OEDIPUS

Child, your talk wins you a pleasure
that will be pain for me. If you have set   1205
your heart on it, so be it.
Only, Theseus: if he is to come here,
let no one have power over my life!

THESEUS

That is the sort of thing I need hear only
once, not twice, old man. I do not boast,
but you should know, your life is safe while mine is.°   1210

(Exit Theseus to the side, with his soldiers, leaving two on guard.)

CHORUS [*singing*]

STROPHE

Though he has watched a decent age pass by,
a man will sometimes still desire the world.
I swear I see no wisdom in that man.
The endless hours pile up a drift of pain
more unrelieved each day; and as for pleasure,
when he is sunken in excessive age   1215
you will not see his pleasure anywhere.
The last attendant is the same for all,
old men and young alike, as in its season   1220
man's heritage of underworld appears:
there being then no epithalamion,
no music and no dance. Death is the finish.

ANTISTROPHE

Not to be born surpasses thought and speech.
The second best is to have seen the light   1225
and then to go back quickly whence we came.
The feathery follies of his youth once over,
what trouble is beyond the range of man?   1230
What heavy burden will he not endure?
Jealousy, faction, quarreling, and battle—
the bloodiness of war, the grief of war.   1235
And in the end he comes to strengthless age,
abhorred by all men, without company,
unfriended in that uttermost twilight
where he must live with every bitter thing.

EPODE

This is the truth, not for me only,

but for this blind and ruined man.   1240
Think of some shore in the north,
the concussive waves make stream
this way and that in the gales of winter:
it is like that with him,
the wild wrack breaking over him
from head to foot, and coming on forever;   1245
now from the plunging down of the sun,
now from the sunrise quarter,
now from where the noonday gleams,
now from the night and the north.

ANTIGONE

I think I see the stranger near us now,
and no men with him, father; but his eyes   1250
swollen with weeping as he comes.

(Enter Polynices, from the side.)

OEDIPUS
                    Who comes?

ANTIGONE

The one whom we have had so long in mind;
it is he who stands here; it is Polynices.

POLYNICES

Ah, now what shall I do? Sisters, shall I
weep for my misfortunes or for those   1255
I see in the old man, my father,
whom I have found here in an alien land,
with two frail girls, an outcast for so long,
and with such garments! The abominable
filth grown old with him, rotting his sides!   1260
And on his sightless face the ragged hair
streams in the wind. There's the same quality
in the food he carries for his thin old belly.
All this I learn too late.

And I swear now that I have been villainous   1265
in not supporting you! You need not wait
to hear it said by others!

     Only, think:
compassion limits even the power of god;°
so may there be a limit with you, father!
For all that has gone wrong may still be healed,   1270
and surely the worst is passed!
Why are you silent?
Speak to me, father! Don't turn away from me!
Will you not answer me at all? Will you
send me away without a word?

                Not even
tell me why you are enraged against me?
Daughters of Oedipus, my own sisters,   1275
try to move your so implacable father;
do not let him reject me in such contempt!
Make him reply! I am here on pilgrimage . . .°

ANTIGONE

Poor brother: you yourself must tell him why.   1280
As men speak on they may sometimes give pleasure,
sometimes annoy, or sometimes touch the heart;
and so somehow provide the mute with voices.

POLYNICES

I will speak out then; your advice is fair.
First, however, I must claim the help   1285
of that same god, Poseidon, from whose altar
the governor of this land has lifted me
and sent me here, giving me leave to speak
and to await response, and a safe passage.
These are the favors I desire from you,
strangers, and from my sisters and my father.   1290
    And now, father, I will tell you why I came.
I am a fugitive, driven from my country,

because I thought fit, as the eldest born,
to take my seat upon your sovereign throne.
For that, Eteocles, the younger of us,   1295
banished me—but not by a decision
in argument or ability or arms;
merely because he won the city over.
Of this I believe the Furies that pursue you
were indeed the cause: and so I hear
from clairvoyants whom I afterward consulted . . .°   1300
Then, when I went to the Dorian land of Argos,
I took Adrastus as my father-in-law,
and bound to me by oath whatever men
were known as leaders or as fighters there;
my purpose being to form an expedition
of seven troops of spearmen against Thebes,   1305
with which enlistment may I die for justice
or else expel the men who exiled me!
     So it is. Then why should I come here now?
Father, my prayers must be made to you,
mine and those of all who fight with me.   1310
Their seven columns under seven captains
even now complete the encirclement of Thebes:
men like Amphiaraus, the hard spear-thrower,
expert in spears and in the ways of eagles;
second is Tydeus, the Aetolian,   1315
son of Oeneus; third is Eteoclus,
born in Argos; fourth is Hippomedon
(his father, Talaus, sent him); Capaneus,
the fifth, has sworn he'll raze the town of Thebes
with fire-brands; and sixth is Parthenopaeus,
an Arcadian who roused himself to war—   1320
son of that virgin famous in the old time
who long years afterward conceived and bore him—
Parthenopaeus, Atalanta's son.
And it is I, your son—or if I am not

truly your son, since evil fathered me,
at least I am called your son—it is I who lead
the fearless troops of Argos against Thebes.   1325
    Now in the name of these two children, father,
and for your own soul's sake, we all implore
and beg you to give up your heavy wrath
against me! I go forth to punish him,
the brother who robbed me of my fatherland.   1330
If we can put any trust in oracles,
they say that those you bless shall come to power.
Now by the gods and fountains of our people,
I pray you, listen and comply! Are we not beggars
both of us, and exiles, you and I?   1335
We live by paying court to other men;
the same fate follows us.
But as for him—how insupportable!—
he lords it in our house, luxuriates there,
laughs at us both!
If you will stand by me in my resolve,   1340
I'll waste no time or trouble whipping him;°
and then I'll reestablish you at home,
and settle there myself, and throw him out.
If your will is the same as mine, it's possible
to promise this. If not, I can't be saved.   1345

CHORUS LEADER

For the sake of the one who sent him, Oedipus,
speak to this man before you send him back.

OEDIPUS

Yes, gentlemen: but were it not Theseus,
the sovereign of your land, who sent him here,
thinking it right that he should have an answer,   1350
you never would have heard a sound from me.
Well: he has asked, and he shall hear from me
a kind of answer that will not overjoy him.
You scoundrel! When it was you who held

throne and authority—as your brother now
holds them in Thebes—you drove me into exile: 1355
me, your own father: made me a homeless man,
insuring me these rags you maunder over°
when you behold them—now that you, as well,
have fallen on evil days and are in exile.
Weeping is no good now. However long 1360
my life may last, I have to see it through;
but I regard you as a murderer!
For you reduced me to this misery;
you made me an exile; because of you
I have begged my daily bread from other men.
If I had not these daughters to sustain me, 1365
I might have lived or died for all your interest.
But they have saved me; they are my support,
and are not girls, but men, in faithfulness.
As for you two, you are no sons of mine!
    And so it is that there are eyes that watch you° 1370
even now; though not as they shall watch
if those troops are in fact marching on Thebes.
You cannot take that city. You'll go down
all bloody,° and your brother, too. For I
have placed that curse upon you before this, 1375
and now I invoke that curse to fight for me,
that you may see a reason to respect
your parents, though your birth was as it was;
and though I am blind, not to dishonor me.
These girls did not.
And so your supplication and your throne 1380
are overmastered surely—if accepted
Justice still has place in the laws of god.°
    Now go! For I abominate and disown you,
wretched scum! Go with the malediction
I here pronounce for you: that you shall never 1385
master your native land by force of arms,
nor ever see your home again in Argos,

the land below the hills; but you shall die
by your own brother's hand, and you shall kill
the brother who banished you. For this I pray.
And I cry out to the hated underworld
that it may take you home; cry out to these   1390
powers indwelling here; and to that power
of furious War that filled your hearts with hate!
Now you have heard me. Go: tell it to Thebes,
tell all the Thebans; tell your faithful fighting
friends what sort of honors   1395
Oedipus has divided among his sons!

CHORUS LEADER
Polynices, I find no matter for sympathy
in your directing yourself here. You may retire.

POLYNICES
Ah, what a journey! What a failure!
My poor companions! See the finish now   1400
of all we marched from Argos for! See me . . .
for I can neither speak of this to anyone
among my friends, nor lead them back again;
I must go silently to meet this doom.
O sisters—daughters of his, sisters of mine!   1405
You heard the hard curse of our father:
for god's sweet sake, if father's curse comes true,
and if you find some way to return home,
do not, at least, dishonor me in death!
But give me a grave and what will quiet me.°   1410
Then you shall have, besides the praise he now
gives you for serving him, an equal praise
for offices you shall have paid my ghost.

ANTIGONE
Polynices, I beseech you, listen to me!

POLYNICES
Dearest—what is it? Tell me, Antigone.   1415

ANTIGONE

Withdraw your troops to Argos as soon as you can.
Do not go to your own death and your city's!

POLYNICES

But that is impossible. How could I command
that army, even backward, once I faltered?

ANTIGONE

Now why, boy, must your anger rise again?   1420
What is the good of laying waste your homeland?

POLYNICES

It is shameful to run; and it is also shameful
to be a laughingstock to a younger brother.

ANTIGONE

But see how you fulfill his prophecies!
Did he not cry that you should kill each other?   1425

POLYNICES

He wishes that. But I cannot give way.

ANTIGONE

Ah, I am desolate! But who will dare
go with you, after hearing the prophecies?

POLYNICES

I'll not report this trifle. A good commander
tells heartening news, or keeps the news to himself.   1430

ANTIGONE

Then you have made up your mind to this, my brother?

POLYNICES

Yes. And do not try to hold me back.
The dark road is before me; I must take it,
doomed by my father and his avenging Furies.
God bless you if you do what I have asked!   1435
It is only in death that you can help me now.°

Now let me go. Good-bye! You will not ever
look in my eyes again.

ANTIGONE

You break my heart!

POLYNICES

Do not grieve for me.

ANTIGONE

Who would not grieve for you,
sweet brother! You go with open eyes to death.   1440

POLYNICES

Death, if that must be.

ANTIGONE

No! Do as I ask!

POLYNICES

You ask the impossible.

ANTIGONE

Then I am lost,
if I must be deprived of you!

POLYNICES

All that
rests with the powers that are over us,
whether it must be so or otherwise.
You two—I pray no evil comes to you;   1445
for all men know you merit no more pain.

(Exit Polynices to the side.)

CHORUS [*singing, while Oedipus and Antigone speak in response*]

STROPHE A

So in this new event we see
new forms of terror working through the blind,
or else inscrutable destiny.   1450
I am not one to say "This is in vain"

of anything allotted to mankind.
Though some must fall, or fall to rise again,
time watches all things steadily— 1455

(A terrific peal of thunder is heard.)

Ah, Zeus! Heaven's height has cracked!

(Thunder and lightning.)

OEDIPUS
O children, children! Could someone here—
could someone bring the hero, Theseus?

ANTIGONE
Father, what is your reason for calling him?

OEDIPUS
Zeus' beating thunder, any moment now, 1460
will clap me underground: send for him quickly!

(Thunder and lightning.)

CHORUS
ANTISTROPHE A
Hear it° cascading down the air!
The god-thrown, the gigantic, holy sound!
Terror crawls to the tips of my hair! 1465
My heart shakes!
There the lightning flames again!
What heavenly marvel is it bringing 'round?
I fear it, for it never comes in vain.
But for man's luck or his despair . . .° 1470

(Another thunderclap.)

STROPHE B
Hear the wild thunder fall!°
Towering Nature is transfixed.
Be merciful, great spirit, if you run 1480
this sword of darkness through our mother land;

come not for our confusion,°
and deal no blows to me,
though your tireless Furies stand
by him whom I have looked upon.
Great Zeus, I make my prayer to you!   1485

OEDIPUS

Is the king near by? Will he come in time
to find me still alive, my mind still clear?

ANTIGONE

Tell me what it is you have in mind!

OEDIPUS

To give him now, in return for his great kindness,
the blessing that I promised I would give.   1490

CHORUS

ANTISTROPHE B

O noble son, return!
No matter if you still descend
in the deep fastness of the sea god's grove,
to make pure offering at his altar fire: 1495
receive from this strange man
whatever may be his heart's desire
that you and I and Athens are worthy of.°
My lord, come quickly as you can!

(Enter Theseus from the side.)

THESEUS

Now why do you all together
set up this shout once more?   1500
I see it comes from you, as from our friend.
Is it a lightning bolt from Zeus? a squall
of rattling hail? Those are familiar things
when such a tempest rages over heaven.

OEDIPUS

My lord, I longed for you to come! This is   1505
gods' work, your lucky coming.

THESEUS

          Now, what new
circumstance has arisen, son of Laius?

OEDIPUS

My life sinks in the scale: I would not die
without fulfilling what I promised Athens.

THESEUS

What proof have you that your hour has come?°   1510

OEDIPUS

The great, incessant thunder and continuous
flashes of lightning from the hand of Zeus.   1515

THESEUS

I believe you. I have seen you prophesy
many things, none falsely. What must be done?

OEDIPUS

I shall disclose to you, O son of Aegeus,
what is appointed for you and for your city:
a thing that age will never wear away.
Presently now, without a soul to guide me,   1520
I'll lead you to the place where I must die;
but you must never tell it to any man,
not even the neighborhood in which it lies.
If you obey, this will count more for you
than many shields and many neighbors' spears.   1525
These things are mysteries, not to be explained;
but you will understand when you come there
alone. Alone, because I cannot disclose it
to any of your men or to my children,
much as I love and cherish them. But you

keep it secret always, and when you come   1530
to the end of life, then you must hand it on
to your most cherished son, and he in turn
must teach it to his heir, and so forever.°
That way you shall forever hold this city
safe from the men of Thebes, the dragon's sons.

    For every nation that lives peaceably,
there will be many others to grow hard
and push their arrogance to extremes. The gods   1535
attend to these things slowly; but they attend
to those who put off god and turn to madness!
You have no mind for that, child of Aegeus.

    Indeed, you know already all that I teach.
Let us now proceed to that place   1540
and hesitate no longer; I am driven
by an insistent voice that comes from god.
Children, follow me this way: see, now,
I have become your guide, as you were mine!
Come: do not touch me: let me alone discover
the holy and funereal ground where I   1545
must take this fated earth to be my shroud.
This way, O come! The angel of the dead,
Hermes, and veiled Persephone lead me on!

       (*Oedipus begins to walk to the side, leading his daughters.*)

O sunlight of no light! Once you were mine!
This is the last my flesh will feel of you;   1550
for now I go to shade my ending day
in the dark underworld. Most cherished friend!
I pray that you and this your land and all
your people may be blessed: remember me.
Be mindful of my death, and be
fortunate in all the time to come!   1555

      (*Exit Oedipus to the side, followed by his daughters*
              and by Theseus with his soldiers.)

CHORUS [*singing*]

STROPHE

If I may dare to adore that lady
the living never see,
and pray to the master of spirits plunged in night,
who of vast Hell has sovereignty:°   1560
let not our friend go down in grief and weariness
to that all-shrouding fold,
the dead man's plain, the house that has no light.
Because his sufferings were great, unmerited and untold,   1565
let some just god relieve him from distress!

ANTISTROPHE

O powers under the earth, and tameless
beast in the passageway,
rumbler prone at the gate of the strange hosts,°   1570
their guard forever, as the legends say:
I pray you, even Death, offspring of Earth and Hell,
to let the descent be clear   1575
as Oedipus goes down among the ghosts
on those dim fields of underground that all men living fear.
Eternal sleep, let Oedipus sleep well!

(Enter a Messenger, from the side.)

MESSENGER
Citizens, the briefest way to tell you
would be to say that Oedipus is no more;   1580
but what has happened cannot be told so simply—
it was no simple thing.

CHORUS LEADER
    He is gone, poor man?

MESSENGER
You may be sure that he has left this world.

CHORUS LEADER
By god's mercy, was his death a painless one?   1585

MESSENGER

That is the thing that seems so marvelous.
You know, for you were witnesses, how he
left this place with no friend leading him,
acting, himself, as guide for all of us.
Well, when he came to the steep place in the road, 1590
the embankment there, secured with steps of brass,
he stopped in one of the many branching paths.
This was not far from the stone bowl that marks
Theseus' and Pirithous' covenant.
Halfway between that place of stone 1595
with its hollow pear tree, and the marble tomb,
he sat down and undid his filthy garments;
then he called his daughters and commanded
that they should bring him water from a fountain
for bathing and libation to the dead.
From there they saw the hillcrest of Demeter, 1600
freshener of all things: they ascended it
and soon came back with water for their father;
then helped him properly to bathe and dress.
When everything was finished to his pleasure
and no command of his remained undone, 1605
then the earth groaned with thunder from the god below;
and as they heard the sound, the girls shuddered
and dropped to their father's knees, and began wailing,
beating their breasts and weeping, as if heartbroken.
And hearing them cry out so bitterly 1610
he put his arms around them, and said to them:
"Children, this day your father is gone from you.
All that was mine is gone. You shall no longer
bear the burden of taking care of me—
I know it was hard, my children. And yet one word
frees us of all the weight and pain of life:° 1615
that word is love. You never shall have more
from anyone than you have had from me.

And now you must spend the rest of life without me."
    That was the way of it. They clung together   1620
and wept, all three. But when they finally stopped
and no more sobs were heard, then there was
silence, and in the silence suddenly
a voice cried out to him—of such a kind
it made our hair stand up in panic fear: 1625
again and again the call came from the god:
"Oedipus! Oedipus! Why are we waiting?
You delay too long; you delay too long to go!"
Then, knowing himself summoned by the spirit,
he asked that the lord Theseus come to him;   1630
and when he had come, said: "O my prince and friend,
give your right hand now as a binding pledge
to my two daughters; children, give him your hands.
Promise that you will never willingly
betray them, but will carry out in kindness
whatever is best for them in the days to come."   1635
And Theseus swore to do it for his friend,
with such restraint as fits a noble king.
And when he had done so, Oedipus at once
laid his blind hands upon his daughters, saying:
"Children, you must show your nobility,°   1640
and have the courage now to leave this spot.
You must not wish to see what is forbidden
or hear such voices as may not be heard.
But go—go quickly. Only the lord Theseus
may stay to see the thing that now begins."
    This much every one of us heard him say,   1645
and then we came away, sobbing, with the girls.
But after a little while as we withdrew
we turned around—and nowhere saw that man,
but only the king, his hands before his face,
shading his eyes as if from something fearful,   1650
awesome and unendurable to see.

Then very quickly we saw him do reverence
to Earth and to the powers of the air,
with one address to both.

But in what manner   1655
Oedipus perished, no one of mortal men
could tell but Theseus. It was not lightning,
bearing its fire from Zeus, that took him off;
no hurricane was blowing.   1660
But some attendant from the train of heaven°
came for him; or else the underworld
opened in love the unlit door of earth.
For he was taken without lamentation,
illness, or suffering; indeed his end
was wonderful if mortal's ever was.   1665
Should someone think I speak intemperately,
I make no apology to him who thinks so.

CHORUS LEADER
But where are his children and the others with them?

MESSENGER
They are not far away; the sound of weeping
should tell you now that they are coming here.

(Enter Antigone and Ismene together, from the side.)

ANTIGONE [*singing in turn with Ismene and the Chorus*]
STROPHE A
Now we may weep, indeed.   1670
Now, if ever, we may cry
in bitter grief against our fate,
our heritage still unappeased.
In other days we stood up under it,
endured it for his sake,
the unrelenting horror. Now the finish
comes, and we know only
in all that we have seen and done   1675
bewildering mystery.

CHORUS

What happened?

ANTIGONE

We can only guess, my friends.

CHORUS

He has gone?

ANTIGONE

He has; as one could wish him to.
Why not? It was not war
nor the deep sea that overtook him,   1680
but something invisible and strange
caught him up—or down—
into a space unseen.
But we are lost, dear sister. A deathly
night is ahead of us.
For how, in some far country wandering,   1685
or on the lifting seas,
shall we eke out our lives?

ISMENE

I cannot guess. But as for me,
I wish that murderous Hades would take me   1690
in one death with our father.
This is such desolation
I cannot go on living.

CHORUS

Most admirable sisters:
whatever god has brought about
is to be borne with courage.
You must not feed the flames of grief;   1695
no blame can come to you.

ANTIGONE

ANTISTROPHE A

One may long for the past

though at the time indeed it seemed
nothing but wretchedness and evil.
Life was not sweet, yet I found it so
when I could put my arms around my father.
O father! O my dear! 1700
Now you are shrouded in eternal darkness.
Even in that absence
you shall not lack our love,
mine and my sister's love.

CHORUS
He lived his life . . .

ANTIGONE
   He did as he had wished!

CHORUS
What do you mean? 1705

ANTIGONE
    In this land among strangers
he died where he chose to die.
He has his eternal bed well shaded
and in his death is not unmourned.
My eyes are blind with tears
from crying for you, father. 1710
The terror and the loss
cannot be quieted.
I know you wished to die in a strange country,
yet your death was so lonely!
Why could I not be with you?

ISMENE
O pity! What is left for me? 1715
What destiny awaits us both
now we have lost our father?°

CHORUS
Dear children, remember 1720

that his last hour was free and blessed.
So make an end of grieving!
Is anyone in all the world
safe from unhappiness?

ANTIGONE

Let us run back there!

ISMENE

Why, what shall we do?

ANTIGONE

I am carried away with longing—   1725

ISMENE

For what—tell me!

ANTIGONE

To see the resting place in the earth—

ISMENE

Of whom?

ANTIGONE

Father's! O, what misery I feel!

ISMENE

But that is not permitted. Do you not see?   1730

ANTIGONE

Do not rebuke me!

ISMENE

And remember, too—

ANTIGONE

Oh, what?

ISMENE

He had no tomb; there was no one near!

ANTIGONE

Take me there and you can kill me, too!

ISMENE

Ah! I am truly lost!

Helpless and so forsaken! 1735

Where shall I go and how shall I live?

CHORUS

ANTISTROPHE B

You must not fear, now.

ANTIGONE

Yes, but where is a refuge?

CHORUS

A refuge has been found—

ANTIGONE

Where do you mean?

CHORUS

A place where you will be unharmed! 1740

ANTIGONE

No . . .

CHORUS

What are you thinking?

ANTIGONE

I think there is no way

for me to get home again.

CHORUS

Do not go home!

ANTIGONE

My home is in trouble.

CHORUS

So it has been before.

ANTIGONE

There was no help for it then: but now it is worse. 1745

CHORUS
A wide and desolate world it is for you.°

ANTIGONE
Great god! What way is there, O Zeus?
Do the powers that rule our lives
still press me on to hope at all?   1750

                    (Enter Theseus from the side, with attendants.)

THESEUS° [*chanting in alternation with Antigone and the Chorus until*
the end of the play]
Mourn no more, children. Those to whom
the night of earth gives benediction
should not be mourned. Retribution comes.

ANTIGONE
Theseus: we fall on our knees to you!

THESEUS
What is it that you desire, children?   1755

ANTIGONE
We wish to see the place ourselves
in which our father rests.

THESEUS
No, no.
It is not permissible to go there.

ANTIGONE
My lord and ruler of Athens, why?

THESEUS
Because your father told me, children,   1760
that no one should go near the spot.
No mortal man should tell of it,
since it is holy, and is his.
And if I kept this pledge, he said,
I should preserve my land from its enemies.   1765

I swore I would, and the god heard me,
the oathkeeper who makes note of all.°

ANTIGONE
If this was our father's cherished wish,
we must be satisfied.
Send us back, then, to ancient Thebes,   1770
in hopes we may stop the bloody war
from coming between our brothers!

THESEUS
I will do that, and whatever else
I am able to do for your happiness,
for his sake who has gone just now   1775
beneath the earth. I must not fail.

CHORUS
Now let the weeping cease;
let no one mourn again.
These things are in the hands of god.°

THE BACCHAE

EURIPIDES
Translated by William Arrowsmith

INTRODUCTION TO EURIPIDES' THE BACCHAE

Euripides wrote *The Bacchae* in the last years of his life during a self-imposed exile in Macedon. It was produced in Athens after his death, which occurred in 406 BCE, and won a posthumous first prize.

Dionysus, on stage disguised as a mortal, is presented as a new god fighting for recognition as a god in the city of his birth, which he thinks should be the first to recognize him yet has fiercely rejected him. Through madness and slaughter he punishes his doubting kinsmen and is established at the end as a god for all the Greeks.

The actual drama is played out as a struggle between two youths, Dionysus and his cousin Pentheus, ruler of Thebes; however, what is important is what Dionysus stands for, not only wine and music, but a new, different kind of religious experience. Accepted, Dionysian religion means pious devotion and joyous liberation; resisted, it will still force its way in, as chaos or madness. The devout Bacchae of the chorus have accepted; the mad women in the hills have had Bacchism forced on them. The utterances of the chorus, as well as those of Teiresias and some of the lower-class characters, constantly go beyond the immediate issues of the action to celebrate a precious and distinctive religious feeling, open to all human beings, barbarians as well as Hellenes, women as well as men, the weak, poor, and unlettered as well as the strong, rich, and wise.

THE BACCHAE

Characters   DIONYSUS (also called Bacchus, Bromius,
Dithyrambus, Euhius, and Iacchus)
CHORUS of Asian Bacchae (female followers of
Dionysus, also called Bacchants and maenads)
TEIRESIAS, Theban seer
CADMUS, father of Semele (Dionysus' mother)
and of Agave
PENTHEUS, king of Thebes
ATTENDANT of Pentheus
FIRST MESSENGER, a shepherd
SECOND MESSENGER, a servant of Pentheus
AGAVE, daughter of Cadmus, mother of
Pentheus

*Scene: Pentheus' palace at Thebes. In front of it stands the tomb of
Semele.*

(Enter Dionysus from the side.)

DIONYSUS
   I am Dionysus, the son of Zeus,
come back to Thebes, this land where I was born.
My mother was Cadmus' daughter, Semele by name,
midwived by fire, delivered by the lightning's
blast.
      And here I stand, a god incognito,
disguised as man, beside the stream of Dirce   5
and the waters of Ismenus. There before the palace

I see my lightning-blasted mother's grave,
and there upon the ruins of her shattered house
the living fire of Zeus still smolders on
in deathless witness of Hera's violence and rage
against my mother. But Cadmus wins my praise: 10
he has made this tomb a shrine, sacred to his daughter.
It was I who screened her grave with the green
of the clustering vine.
               Far behind me lie
the gold-rich lands of Lydia and Phrygia,
where my journeying began. Overland I went,
across the steppes of Persia where the sun strikes hotly
down, through Bactrian fastness and the grim waste   15
of Media. Thence to blessed Arabia I came;
and so, along all Asia's swarming littoral
of towered cities where barbarians and Greeks,
mingling, live, my progress made. There
I taught my dances to the feet of living men,
establishing my mysteries and rites
that I might be revealed to mortals for what I am:
a god.
       And thence to Thebes.
                     This city, first   20
in Hellas, now shrills and echoes to my women's cries,
their ecstasy of joy. Here in Thebes
I bound the fawnskin to the women's flesh and armed
their hands with shafts of ivy. For I have come   25
to refute that slander spoken by my mother's sisters—
those who least had right to slander her.
They said that Dionysus was no son of Zeus,
but Semele had slept beside a man in love
and foisted off her shame on Zeus—a fraud, they sneered,   30
contrived by Cadmus to protect his daughter's name.
They said she lied, and Zeus in anger at that lie
blasted her with lightning.

Because of that offense
I have stung them with frenzy, hounded them from home
up to the mountains where they wander, crazed of mind,
and compelled them to wear my ritual uniform.
Every woman in Thebes—but the women only—   35
I drove from home, mad. There they sit,
all of them, together with the daughters of Cadmus,
beneath the silver firs on the roofless rocks.
Like it or not, this city must learn its lesson:
it lacks initiation in my mysteries;   40
so I shall vindicate my mother Semele
and stand revealed to mortal eyes as the god
she bore to Zeus.
                Cadmus the king has abdicated,
leaving his throne and power to his grandson Pentheus,
who revolts against divinity, in me;   45
thrusts me from his offerings; omits my name
from his prayers. Therefore I shall prove to him
and everyone in Thebes that I am god
indeed. And when my worship is established here,
and all is well, then I shall go my way
and be revealed to other men in other lands.   50
But if the town of Thebes attempts to force
my Bacchae from the mountainside with weapons,
I shall marshal my maenads and take the field.
To these ends I have laid divinity aside
and go disguised as man.

                                    (Calling toward the side.)

                    On, my women,   55
women who worship me, women whom I led
out of Asia where Tmolus heaves its rampart
over Lydia!
                On, comrades of my progress here!
Come, and with your native Phrygian drum—

Rhea's invention and mine—pound at the doors   60
of Pentheus' palace! Let the city of Thebes behold you,
while I myself go to Cithaeron's glens
where my Bacchae wait, and join their whirling dances.

(*Exit Dionysus to one side. Enter the Chorus
of Asian Bacchae from the other.*)

CHORUS [*singing*]
Out of the land of Asia,
down from holy Tmolus,   65
speeding the god's service,
for Bromius we come!
Hard are the labors of god;
hard, but his service is sweet.
Sweet to serve, sweet to cry:

Bacchus! Euhoi!

You on the streets! You on the roads!
You in the palace! Come out!
Let every mouth be hushed.   70
Let no ill-omened words
profane your tongues.
For now I shall raise the old, old hymn to Dionysus.

STROPHE A
Blessed, those who know the god's mysteries,°
happy those who sanctify their lives,
whose souls are initiated into the holy company,   75
dancing on the mountains the holy dance of the god,
and those who keep the rites of Cybele the Mother,
and who shake the thyrsus,   80
who wear the crown of ivy.
Dionysus is their god!
On, Bacchae, on, you Bacchae,
bring the god, son of god,
bring Bromius home,   85
from Phrygian mountains,
to the broad streets of Hellas—Bromius!

ANTISTROPHE A

His mother bore him once in labor bitter;
lightning-struck, forced by fire that flared from Zeus,   90
consumed, she died, untimely torn,
in childbed dead by blow of light!
Zeus it was who saved his son,   95
swiftly bore him to a private place,
concealed his son from Hera's eyes
in his thigh as in a womb,
binding it with clasps of gold.
And when the weaving Fates fulfilled the time,   100
the bull-horned god was born of Zeus.
He crowned his son with garlands,
wherefrom descends to us the maenad's writhing crown,
wild creatures in our hair.

STROPHE B

O Thebes, nurse of Semele,   105
    crown your head with ivy!
    Grow green with bryony!
    Redden with berries! O city,
    with boughs of oak and fir,   110
    come dance the dance of god!
    Fringe your skins of dappled fawn
    with tufts of twisted wool!
    Handle with holy care
    the violent wand of god!
And at once the whole land shall dance
when Bromius leads the holy company   115
to the mountain!
                to the mountain!
where the throng of women waits,
driven from shuttle and loom,
possessed by Dionysus!

ANTISTROPHE B

And I praise the holies of Crete,   120

the caves of the dancing Curetes,
there where Zeus was born,
where helmed in triple tier
the Corybantes invented this leather drum.　　125
They were the first of all
whose whirling feet kept time
to the strict beat of the taut hide
and the sweet cry of the Phrygian pipes.
Then from them to Rhea's hands
the holy drum was handed down,
to give the beat for maenads' dances;
and, taken up by the raving satyrs,　　130
it now accompanies the dance
which every other year
celebrates your name:
　　　　Dionysus!

EPODE

He is sweet upon the mountains, when he drops to the earth　　135
　　　　from the running packs.
He wears the holy fawnskin. He hunts the wild goat
　　　　and kills it.
He delights in raw flesh.
He runs to the mountains of Phrygia, of Lydia,　　140
Bromius, who leads us! Euhoi!
　　　　With milk the earth flows! It flows with wine!
It runs with the nectar of bees!
　　　　Like frankincense in its fragrance
is the blaze of the torch he bears,　　145
flaming from his trailing fennel wand
　　　　as he runs, as he dances,
kindling the stragglers,
　　　　spurring with cries,
and his long curls stream to the wind!　　150
And he cries, as they cry,°
　　　　"On, Bacchae!

> *On, Bacchae!*
> *Follow, glory of golden Tmolus,*
>   *hymning Dionysus*   155
>   *with a rumble of drums,*
>   *with the cry, Euhoi! to the Euhoian god,*
> *with cries in Phrygian melodies,*
> *when the holy pipe like honey plays*   160
> *the sacred song for those who go*
> *to the mountain!*
>   *to the mountain!"*   165
> *Then, in ecstasy, like a colt by its grazing mother,*
> *the bacchant runs with flying feet, she leaps!*

(Enter Teiresias from the side, dressed in the bacchant's
fawnskin and ivy crown, and carrying a thyrsus.)

TEIRESIAS

Ho there, who keeps the gates?
                           Summon Cadmus—   170
Cadmus, Agenor's son, who came from Sidon
and built the towers of our Thebes.
                           Go, someone.
Say Teiresias wants him. He will know what errand
brings me, that agreement, age with age, we made   175
to deck our wands, to dress in skins of fawn
and crown our heads with ivy.

(Enter Cadmus from the palace, dressed like Teiresias.)

CADMUS

                        My old friend,
I knew it must be you when I heard your summons.
For there's a wisdom in his voice that makes
the man of wisdom known.
                        So here I am,
dressed in the costume of the god, prepared to go.   180
Insofar as we are able, Teiresias, we must
do honor to this god, for he was born

my daughter's son, who has been revealed to men,°
the god, Dionysus.

Where shall we go, where
shall we tread the dance, tossing our white-haired heads
in the dances of the god?

Expound to me, Teiresias,   185
age to age: for you are wise.

Surely
I could dance night and day, untiringly
beating the earth with my thyrsus! And how sweet it is
to forget my old age.

TEIRESIAS

It is the same with me.
I too feel young, young enough to dance.   190

CADMUS

Good. Shall we not take our chariots to the mountain?

TEIRESIAS

Walking would be better. It shows more honor
to the god.

CADMUS

So be it. I shall lead, my old age
conducting yours.

TEIRESIAS

The god will guide us there
with no effort on our part.

CADMUS

Are we the only men   195
who will dance for Bacchus?

TEIRESIAS

The others are all blind.
Only we can see.

CADMUS

                But we delay too long.
Here, take my arm.

TEIRESIAS

                Link my hand in yours.

CADMUS

I am a man, nothing more. I do not scoff
at gods.

TEIRESIAS

                We do not trifle with divinity.°   200
No, we are the heirs of customs and traditions
hallowed by age and handed down to us
by our fathers. No quibbling logic can topple them,
whatever subtleties this clever age invents.
People may say: "Aren't you ashamed? At your age,
going dancing, wreathing your head with ivy?"   205
Well, I am not ashamed. Did the god declare
that just the young or just the old should dance?
No, he desires his honor from all mankind.
He wants no one excluded from his worship.

CADMUS

Because you cannot see, Teiresias, let me be   210
interpreter for you this time. Here comes
the man to whom I left my throne, Echion's son,
Pentheus, hastening toward the palace. He seems
excited and disturbed. What is his news?

                            (Enter Pentheus from the side.)

PENTHEUS

I happened to be away, out of this land,   215
but I've heard of some strange mischief in the town,
stories of our women leaving home to frisk
in mock ecstasies among the thickets on the mountain,

dancing in honor of the latest divinity,
a certain Dionysus, whoever he may be!   220
In their midst stand bowls brimming with wine.
And then, one by one, the women wander off
to hidden nooks where they serve the lusts of men.
Priestesses of Bacchus they claim they are,
but it's really Aphrodite they adore.   225
I have captured some of them; my jailers
have bound their hands and locked them in our prison.
Those who run at large shall be hunted down
out of the mountains like the animals they are—
yes, my own mother Agave, and Ino
and Autonoë, the mother of Actaeon.   230
In no time at all I shall have them trapped
in iron nets and stop this obscene disorder.

    I am also told a foreigner has come to Thebes
from Lydia, one of those charlatan magicians,
with long yellow curls smelling of perfumes,   235
with flushed cheeks and the spells of Aphrodite
in his eyes. His days and nights he spends
with women and girls, dangling before them the joys
of initiation in his mysteries.
But let me catch him in this land of mine
and I'll stop his pounding with his wand and tossing   240
his head. I'll have his head cut off his body!
And *this* is the man who claims that Dionysus
is a god and was sewn into the thigh of Zeus,
when, in point of fact, that same blast of lightning
consumed him and his mother both, for her lie   245
that she had lain with Zeus in love. Whoever
this stranger is, aren't such impostures,
such unruliness, worthy of hanging?

                       (He catches sight of Teiresias and Cadmus.)

                What!
But this is incredible! Teiresias the seer

tricked out in a dappled fawnskin!
                    And you,
you, my grandfather, playing the bacchant—what a laugh!—   250
with a fennel wand!
                    Sir, I shrink to see your old age
so foolish. Shake that ivy off, grandfather!
Now drop that wand. Drop it, I say.
                    Aha,
I see: this is your doing, Teiresias.   255
Yes, you want still another god revealed to men
so you can pocket the profits from burnt offerings
and bird-watching. By heaven, only your age
restrains me now from sending you to prison
with those Bacchic women for importing here to Thebes
these filthy mysteries. When once you see   260
the glint of wine shining at the feasts of women,
then you may be sure the festival is rotten.

CHORUS LEADER
What blasphemy! Stranger, have you no respect
for the gods? For Cadmus who sowed the dragon teeth?
Will the son of Echion disgrace his house?   265

TEIRESIAS
Give a wise man an honest brief to plead
and his eloquence is no remarkable achievement.
But you are glib; your phrases come rolling out
smoothly on the tongue, as though your words were wise
instead of foolish. The man whose glibness flows
from his conceit of speech declares the thing he is: 270
a worthless and a stupid citizen.
                        I tell you,
this god whom you ridicule shall someday have
enormous power and prestige throughout Hellas.
Mankind, young man, possesses two supreme blessings.
First of these is the goddess Demeter, or Earth—   275
whichever name you choose to call her by.

It was she who gave to man his nourishment of dry food.
But after her there came the son of Semele,
who matched her present by inventing liquid wine
from grapes as his gift to man. For filled with juice from
    vines,
suffering mankind forgets its grief; from it   280
comes sleep; with it oblivion of the troubles
of the day. There is no other medicine
for misery. And when we pour libations
to the gods, we pour the god of wine himself
that through his intercession man may win   285
the good things of life.
                    You sneer, do you, at that story
that Dionysus was sewn into the thigh of Zeus?
Let me teach you what that really means. When Zeus
rescued from the thunderbolt his infant son,
he brought him to Olympus. Hera, however,
plotted at heart to hurl the child from heaven.   290
Like the god he is, Zeus countered her. Breaking off
a tiny fragment of that ether which surrounds the earth,
he molded from it a substitute Dionysus.
This piece of "sky" he gave to Hera as a hostage,
and thereby saved Dionysus from Hera's hate. With time,
men garbled the word and said that he'd been sewn   295
into the "thigh" of Zeus. This was their story,
whereas, in fact, Zeus made a fake for Hera
and gave it as a hostage for his son.
                                Moreover,
this is a god of prophecy. His worshippers,
like maniacs, are endowed with mantic powers.
For when the god goes greatly into a man,   300
he drives him mad and makes him tell the future.
                                Besides,
he has usurped even some functions of warlike Ares.
Thus, at times, you see an army mustered under arms
stricken with panic before it lifts a spear.

This panic comes from Dionysus.
                          Someday   305
you shall even see him bounding with his torches
among the crags at Delphi, leaping the pastures
that stretch between the peaks, whirling and waving
his thyrsus: great throughout Hellas.
                          Mark my words,
Pentheus. Don't be so sure that domination   310
is what matters in the life of man; do not mistake
for wisdom the fantasies of a sick mind.
Welcome the god to Thebes; crown your head;
pour him libations and join his revels.

       Dionysus does not, I admit, compel a woman
to be chaste.° Always and in every case   315
it is her character and nature that keep°
a woman chaste. But even in the rites of Dionysus,
the chaste woman will not be corrupted.
                          Think:
you are pleased when men stand outside your doors
and the city glorifies the name of Pentheus.   320
And so the god: he too delights in honor.
So Cadmus, whom you ridicule, and I will crown
our heads with ivy and join the dances of the god—
an ancient gray-haired pair perhaps, but dance
we must. Nothing you have said would make me
change my mind or fight against a god.   325
You are mad, grievously mad, beyond the power
of any drugs to cure, for you are drugged
with madness.

CHORUS LEADER
                          Apollo would approve your words.
Wisely you honor Bromius: a great god.

CADMUS
                          My boy,
Teiresias advises well. Your home is here   330

with us, with our customs and traditions, not
outside, alone. You flit about, and though
you may be smart, your smartness is all nothing.
Even if this Dionysus is no god,
as you assert, persuade yourself that he is.
The falsehood is a noble one, for Semele will seem   335
to be the mother of a god, and this confers
no small distinction on our family.

          You see
that dreadful death your cousin Actaeon died
when those man-eating hounds he had raised himself
savaged him and tore his body limb from limb
because he boasted that his prowess in the hunt surpassed   340
the skill of Artemis.

        Do not let his fate be yours.
Here, let me wreathe your head with leaves of ivy.
Then come with us and glorify the god.

PENTHEUS

Take your hands off me! Go worship your Bacchus,
but do not wipe your madness off on me.
By god, I'll make him pay, the man who taught you   345
this folly of yours.

         (To his attendants.)

       Go, someone, this instant,
to the place where this prophet prophesies.
Pry it up with crowbars, heave it over,
upside down; demolish everything you see.
Throw his fillets out to wind and weather.   350
That will provoke him more than anything.

       (Exit an attendant to one side.)

As for you others, go and scour the city
for that effeminate stranger, the man who infects our women
with this new disease and pollutes their beds.

And if you catch him, clap him in chains   355
and march him here. He shall die as he deserves—
by being stoned to death. He shall come to rue
his merrymaking here in Thebes.

> *(Exit other attendants to the other side.)*

TEIRESIAS
                                        Reckless fool,
you do not know the meaning of what you say.
You were out of your mind before, but this is raving
lunacy!
                        Cadmus, let us go and pray   360
for this crazed fool and for this city too,
pray to the god that he take no vengeance
upon us.
                        Take your staff and follow me.
Support me with your hands, and I shall help you too
lest we stumble and fall, a sight of shame,
two old men together.
                        But go we must,   365
acknowledging the service that we owe to god,
Bacchus, the son of Zeus.
                        And yet take care
lest someday your house repent of Pentheus
for its sufferings. I speak not prophecy
but fact. The words of fools finish in folly.

> *(Exit Teiresias and Cadmus to the side.)*

CHORUS [*singing*]
                        STROPHE A
Holiness, queen of heaven,   370
    Holiness on golden wing
    who fly over the earth,
    do you hear what Pentheus says?
    Do you hear his blasphemy
    against the prince of the blessèd,   375

the god of garlands and banquets,
Bromius, Semele's son?
These blessings he gave:
the sacred company's dance and song,
laughter to the pipe   380
and the loosing of cares
when the shining wine is poured
at the feast for the gods,
and the wine bowl casts its sleep   385
on feasters crowned with ivy.

ANTISTROPHE A

A tongue without reins,
defiance, unwisdom—
their end is disaster.
But the life of quiet good,
the wisdom that accepts—   390
these abide unshaken,
preserving, sustaining
the houses of men.
Far in the air of heaven,
the sons of heaven live.
But they watch the lives of men.
And what passes for wisdom is not;   395
unwise those who outrange mortal limits.
Briefly, we live. Wherefore
he who hunts great things
may lose his harvest here and now.
I say: such men are mad,   400
their counsels evil.

STROPHE B

O let me go to Cyprus,
island of Aphrodite,
home of the Loves that cast
their spells on the hearts of men!   405

Or Paphos where the hundred-
mouthed barbarian river
brings ripeness without rain!
To loveliest Pieria, haunt of the Muses,   410
the holy hill of Olympus!
O Bromius, leader, god of joy,
Bromius, take me there!
There the lovely Graces are,
and there Desire, and there
the bacchants have the right to worship.   415

ANTISTROPHE B

The deity, the son of Zeus,
in feast, in festival, delights.
He loves the goddess Peace,
generous of good,
preserver of the young.   420
To rich and poor he gives
the painless delight of wine.
But him he hates who scoffs
at the happiness of those
for whom the day is blessed   425
and blessed the night;
whose simple wisdom shuns the thoughts°
of proud, uncommon men.
What the common people   430
believe and do,
I too believe and do.

(Enter Dionysus from the side, led captive by several attendants.)

ATTENDANT

Pentheus, here we are; not empty-handed either.
We captured the quarry you sent us out to catch.   435
Our prey here was quite tame: refused to run,
but just held out his hands as willing as you please,

completely unafraid. His wine-red cheeks were flushed
and did not pale at all. He stood there smiling,
telling us to rope his hands and march him here.   440
That made things easy—and it made me feel ashamed.
"Listen, stranger," I said, "I am not to blame.
We act under orders from Pentheus. He ordered
your arrest."

        As for those bacchants you clapped in chains
and sent to the prison, they're gone, clean away,   445
went skipping off to the fields crying on their god
Bromius. The chains on their legs snapped apart
by themselves. Untouched by any human hand,
the doors swung wide, opening of their own accord.
Sir, this stranger who has come to Thebes is full   450
of many miracles. I know no more than that.
The rest is your affair.

PENTHEUS

        Untie his hands.
We have him in our net. He may be quick,
but he cannot escape us now, I think.

                        (The attendants do as instructed.)

        So,
you are attractive, stranger, at least to women—
which explains, I think, your presence here in Thebes.
Your curls are long; they fall along your cheeks.
You do not wrestle, I take it. And what fair skin!   455
You must take care of it—not in the sun, by night
when you hunt Aphrodite with your beauty.
        Now then,
what country do you come from?

DIONYSUS

        It is nothing   460
to boast of and easily told. You have heard, I suppose,
of Mount Tmolus and her flowers?

PENTHEUS

I know of the place.
It rings the city of Sardis.

DIONYSUS

I come from there.
My country is Lydia.

PENTHEUS

And from where comes this cult
you have imported into Hellas?

DIONYSUS

Dionysus, the son of Zeus.   465
He initiated me.

PENTHEUS

You have some local Zeus there
who spawns new gods?

DIONYSUS

He is the same as yours:
the Zeus who married Semele.

PENTHEUS

How did you see him?
In a dream or face to face?

DIONYSUS

Face to face.
He gave me his rites.

PENTHEUS

What form do they take,   470
these rituals of yours?

DIONYSUS

It is forbidden
to tell the uninitiate.

PENTHEUS

Tell me the benefits
that those who know your mysteries enjoy.

DIONYSUS

You're not allowed to hear. But they are worth knowing.

PENTHEUS

Your answers are designed to make me curious.

DIONYSUS

No: 475
our mysteries abhor an unbelieving man.

PENTHEUS

You say you saw the god. What form did he assume?

DIONYSUS

Whatever form he wished. The choice was his,
not mine.

PENTHEUS

You evade the question.

DIONYSUS

Talk sense to a fool
and he calls you foolish.

PENTHEUS

Have you introduced your rites 480
in other cities too? Or is Thebes the first?

DIONYSUS

Barbarians everywhere now dance for Dionysus.

PENTHEUS

They are more ignorant than Greeks.

DIONYSUS

In this matter
they are not. Customs differ.

PENTHEUS

                    Do you hold your rites
during the day or night?

DIONYSUS

                    Mostly by night.   485
The darkness is well suited to devotion.

PENTHEUS

Better suited to lechery and seducing women.

DIONYSUS

You can find debauchery by daylight too.

PENTHEUS

You shall regret these clever answers.

DIONYSUS

                    And you,
your stupid blasphemies.

PENTHEUS

                    What a bold bacchant!   490
You wrestle well—when it comes to words.

DIONYSUS

                    Tell me,
what punishment do you propose?

PENTHEUS

                    First of all,
I shall cut off your girlish curls.

DIONYSUS

                    My hair is holy.
My curls belong to god.

                    (*Pentheus shears away some of the god's curls.*)

PENTHEUS

                    Second, you will surrender
your wand.

DIONYSUS

You take it. It belongs to Dionysus.   495

(Pentheus takes the thyrsus.)

PENTHEUS

Last, I shall place you under guard and confine you
in the palace.

DIONYSUS

The god himself will set me free
whenever I wish.

PENTHEUS

You will be with your women in prison
when you call on him for help.

DIONYSUS

He is here now
and sees what I endure from you.

PENTHEUS

Where is he?   500
My eyes don't see him.

DIONYSUS

With me. Your blasphemies
have made you blind.

PENTHEUS   *(To attendants.)*
Seize him. He is mocking me
and Thebes.

DIONYSUS

And I say, Don't chain me up! I am sane
but you are not.

PENTHEUS

But I say: chain him.
And I'm the ruler here.

DIONYSUS

You do not know   505

what is the life you live.° You do not know

what you do. You do not know who you are.

PENTHEUS

I am Pentheus, the son of Echion and Agave.

DIONYSUS

Pentheus: you shall repent that name.

PENTHEUS

Off with him.

Chain his hands; lock him in the stables by the palace.

Since he desires the darkness, give him what he wants.   510

Let him dance down there in the dark.

As for these women,

your accomplices in making trouble here,

I shall have them sold as slaves or put to work

at my looms. That will silence their drums.

DIONYSUS

I go,   515

for I won't suffer what I'm not meant to suffer.

But Dionysus whom you outrage by your acts,

who you deny is god, will call you to account.

You mistreat me—but it's he you drag to prison.

(Exit Pentheus, Dionysus, and attendants into the palace.)

CHORUS [singing]

STROPHE

O Dirce, holy river,   520

child of Achelous' water,

yours the springs that welcomed once

divinity, the son of Zeus!

For Zeus his father snatched him in his thigh

from deathless flame, crying: 525

Dithyrambus, come!
Enter my male womb.
I name you, Bacchius, and to Thebes
proclaim you by that name.
But now, O blessed Dirce,   530
you spurn me when to your banks I come,
crowned with ivy, bringing revels.
O Dirce, why do you reject me? Why do you flee me?
By the clustered grapes I swear,
by Dionysus' wine,   535
someday you shall come to know
        the worship of Bromius!

ANTISTROPHE

Pentheus, son of Echion,°   540
    shows he was born of the breed of Earth,
    spawned by the dragon, whelped by Earth,
    inhuman, a rabid beast,
    a Giant in wildness,
    defying the children of heaven.
He will fetter me soon,   545
me, who belong to Bromius!
He cages my comrades with chains;
he has cast them in prison darkness.
O lord, son of Zeus, do you see?   550
O Dionysus, do you see
how your spokesmen are wrestling with compulsion?
Descend from Olympus, lord!
Come, whirl your wand of gold
and quell the violence of this murderous man!   555

EPODE

O lord, where do you brandish your wand
    among the holy companies?
    There on Nysa, mother of beasts?
    There on the ridges of Corycia?
    Or there among the forests of Olympus   560

where Orpheus fingered his lyre
and mustered with music the trees,
mustered the wilderness beasts?
O Pieria, you are blessed!   565
Euhius honors you. He will come to dance,
bringing his Bacchae, crossing the swift rivers
Axios and Lydias,   570
generous father of wealth
and famed, I hear, for his lovely waters
that fatten a land of good horses.   575

(In the following scene, sounds of thunder, lightning,
and earthquake are heard from offstage.)

DIONYSUS [*singing from within in this lyric interchange with the*
Chorus, who sing in reply]
  Ho!
  Hear me! Ho, Bacchae!
  Ho, Bacchae! Hear my cry!

CHORUS
  Who cries?
  Who calls me with that cry
  of Euhius?

DIONYSUS
  Ho! Again I cry—   580
  I, the son of Zeus and Semele!

CHORUS
  O lord, lord Bromius!
  Bromius, come to our holy company now!

DIONYSUS
  Let the earthquake come! Shatter° the floor of the world!   585

CHORUS
  Look there, soon the palace of Pentheus will totter.
  Dionysus is within. Adore him!

We adore him!　　　　　　　　　　　　　　　　　　　590
Look there!
　　　　Above the pillars, how the great stones
　　gape and crack!
　　　　　Listen. Bromius cries his victory!

DIONYSUS

Launch the blazing thunderbolt of god!
Consume with flame the palace of Pentheus!　　　　595

CHORUS

Ah,
look how the fire leaps up
on the holy tomb of Semele,
the flame of Zeus of Thunders,
his lightnings, still alive!
Down, maenads,　　　　　　　　　　　　　　　600
throw to the ground your trembling bodies!
Our lord attacks this palace,
turns it upside down,
the son of Zeus!

　　　　　　　　(The Chorus falls to the ground in terror and
　　　　　　　　veneration. Enter Dionysus from the palace.)

DIONYSUS [*speaking*]

What's this, women of Asia? So overcome with fright
that you fell to the ground? I think you must have heard　　605
how Bacchius jostled the palace of Pentheus. But come, rise.°
Do not be afraid.

CHORUS LEADER

　　　　　O greatest light of our holy revels,
how glad I am to see your face! Without you I was lost.

DIONYSUS

Did you despair when they led me away to cast me down　　610
in the darkness of Pentheus' prison?

CHORUS LEADER
        What else could I do?
Where would I turn for help if something happened to you?
But how did you escape that godless man?

DIONYSUS
        No problem.
I saved myself with ease.

CHORUS LEADER
        But the manacles on your wrists?   615

DIONYSUS
There I, in turn, humiliated him, outrage for outrage.
He seemed to think that he was chaining me but never once
so much as touched my hands. He fed upon his hopes.
Inside the stable he intended as my jail, instead of me,
he found a bull and tried to rope its knees and hooves.
He was panting desperately, biting his lips with his teeth,   620
his whole body drenched with sweat, while I sat nearby,
quietly watching. But at that moment Bacchus came,
shook the palace and lit his mother's grave with tongues
of fire. Imagining the palace was in flames,
Pentheus went rushing here and there, shouting to his slaves   625
to bring him water. Every hand was put to work: in vain.
Then, afraid I had escaped, he suddenly stopped short,
drew his sword and rushed to the palace. There, it seems,
Bromius had made a phantom—at least it seemed to me—   630
within the court. Pursuing, Pentheus thrust and stabbed
at that thing of gleaming air° as though he were killing me.
And then, once again, Bacchius humiliated him.
He razed the palace to the ground where it lies, shattered
in utter ruin—his reward for my imprisonment.
At that bitter sight, Pentheus dropped his sword, exhausted   635
by the struggle. A man, a man, and nothing more,
yet he presumed to wage a war with god.

For my part,
I left the palace quietly and made my way outside.
For Pentheus I care nothing.

But judging from the sound
of tramping feet inside the court, I think our man
will soon come out. What, I wonder, will he have to say?   640
But let him bluster. I shall not be touched to rage.
Wise men know constraint: our passions are controlled.

(Enter Pentheus from the palace.)

PENTHEUS

What has happened to me is monstrous! That stranger, that
    man
I clapped in irons, has escaped.

(He catches sight of Dionysus.)

What! You?   645
Well, what do you have to say for yourself?
How did you escape? Answer me.

DIONYSUS

Your anger
walks too heavily. Tread lightly here.

PENTHEUS

How did you escape?

DIONYSUS

Don't you remember?
Someone, I said, would set me free.

PENTHEUS

Someone?   650
But who? The things you say are always strange.

DIONYSUS

He who makes the grape grow its clusters
for mankind.

PENTHEUS

His chiefest glory is his reproach.°

DIONYSUS

The god himself will come to teach you wisdom.

PENTHEUS

I hereby order every gate in every tower
to be bolted tight.

(Exit some attendants to the sides.)

DIONYSUS

And so? Could not a god
hurdle your city walls?

PENTHEUS

You are clever—very—   655
but not where it counts.

DIONYSUS

Where it counts the most,
there I am clever.

(Enter a herdsman as Messenger from the side.)

But hear this messenger
who brings you news from the mountain of Cithaeron.
I shall remain where we are. Do not fear:
I will not run away.

MESSENGER

Pentheus, king of Thebes,   660
I come from Cithaeron where the gleaming flakes of snow
fall on and on forever.

PENTHEUS

Get to the point.
What is your message, man?

MESSENGER

Sir, I have seen

the holy maenads, the women who ran barefoot 665
and crazy from the city, and I wanted to report
to you and Thebes what strange fantastic things,
what miracles and more than miracles,
these women do. But may I speak freely
of what happened there, or should I trim my words?
I fear the harsh impatience of your nature, sire, 670
too kingly and too quick to anger.

PENTHEUS
                    Speak freely.
You have my promise: I shall not punish you.
Displeasure with a man of justice is not right.°
However, the more terrible this tale of yours,
that much more terrible will be the punishment 675
I impose upon this man who taught our womenfolk
these strange new skills.

MESSENGER
                    About that hour
when the sun sends forth its light to warm the earth,
our grazing herds of cows had just begun to climb
the path along the mountain ridge. Suddenly
I saw three companies of women dancers, 680
one led by Autonoë, the second captained
by your mother Agave, while Ino led the third.
There they lay in the deep sleep of exhaustion,
some resting on boughs of fir, others sleeping
where they fell, here and there among the oak leaves— 685
but all modestly and soberly, not, as you think,
drunk with wine, nor wandering, led astray
by the music of the pipe, to hunt their Aphrodite
through the woods.
                    But your mother heard the lowing
of our hornèd herds, and springing to her feet, 690
gave a great cry to waken them from sleep.
And they too, rubbing the bloom of deep sleep

from their eyes, rose up lightly and straight—
a lovely sight to see: all together in fine order,
the old women and the young and the unmarried girls.
First they let their hair fall loose, down   695
over their shoulders, and those whose fastenings had slipped
closed up their skins of fawn with writhing snakes
that licked their cheeks. Breasts swollen with milk,
new mothers who had left their babies behind at home
nestled gazelles and young wolves in their arms,   700
suckling them. Then they crowned their hair with leaves,
ivy and oak and flowering bryony. One woman
struck her thyrsus against a rock and a fountain
of cool water came bubbling up. Another drove   705
her fennel in the ground, and where it struck the earth,
at the god's touch, a spring of wine poured out.
Those who wanted milk scratched at the soil
with bare fingers and the white milk came welling up.   710
Pure honey spurted, streaming, from their wands.
If you had been there and seen these wonders for yourself,
you'd surely yourself have approached with fervent prayers
the god you now deny.
                    We cowherds and shepherds
gathered together, wondering and arguing   715
among ourselves at these fantastic things,
the awesome miracles those women did.°
But then a city fellow with the knack of words
rose to his feet and said: "All you who live
upon the pastures of the mountain, what do you say?
Shall we earn a little favor with King Pentheus   720
by hunting his mother Agave out of the revels?"
Falling in with his suggestion, we withdrew
and set ourselves in ambush, hidden by the leaves
among the undergrowth. At the appointed time
the bacchants began to shake their wands in worship
of Bacchus. With one voice they cried aloud:
"O Iacchus! Son of Zeus!" "O Bromius!" they cried   725

until the beasts and all the mountain were
wild with divinity. And when they ran,
everything ran with them.

            It happened, however,
that Agave ran near the ambush where I lay
concealed. Leaping up, I tried to seize her,   730
but she gave a cry: "Hounds who run with me,
men are hunting us down! Follow, follow me!
Use your wands for weapons."

            At this we fled
and barely escaped being torn to pieces by the women.
Unarmed, they swooped down upon the herds of cattle   735
grazing there on the green of the meadow. And then
you could have seen a single woman with bare hands
tear a fat calf, still bellowing with fright,
in two, while others clawed the heifers to pieces.
There were ribs and cloven hooves scattered everywhere,   740
and scraps smeared with blood hung from the fir trees.
And bulls, their raging fury gathered in their horns,
lowered their heads to charge, then fell, stumbling
to the earth, pulled down by hordes of women   745
and stripped of flesh and skin more quickly, sire,
than you could blink your royal eyes. Then,
carried up by their own speed, they flew like birds
across the spreading fields along Asopus' stream
where the rich soil yields plentiful grain for Thebes.   750
Like invaders they swooped on Hysiae
and on Erythrae in the foothills of Cithaeron.
Everything in sight they pillaged and destroyed.
They snatched the children from their homes. And see—
    whatever
they piled as plunder on their shoulders stayed in place,   755
untied. Nothing, neither bronze nor iron,
fell to the dark earth.° They were carrying fire
in their hair—it did not burn them. Then the villagers,
furious at what the Bacchae did, took to arms.

And there, sire, was something terrible to see.   760
For the men's spears were pointed and sharp, and yet
drew no blood, whereas the wands the women threw
inflicted wounds. And then the men ran,
routed by women! Some god, I say, was with them.
The women then returned where they had started,   765
by the springs the god had made, and washed their hands
while the snakes licked away the drops of blood
that dabbled their cheeks.
                    Whoever this god may be,
sire, welcome him to Thebes. For he is great
in many ways, but above all it was he,   770
or so they say, who gave to mortal men
the gift of lovely wine by which our suffering
is stopped. And if there is no god of wine,
there is no love, no Aphrodite either,
nor other pleasure left to men.

                                        (*Exit Messenger to the side.*)

CHORUS LEADER
                            I tremble   775
to speak my words in freedom before a tyrant.
But nonetheless I'll say: there is no god
greater than Dionysus.

PENTHEUS
                            Like a blazing fire
this Bacchic violence spreads. It comes too close.
We are disgraced, humiliated in the eyes
of Hellas. This is no time for hesitation.   780

                                        (*To an attendant.*)

You there. Go down quickly to the Electran gates
and order out all heavy-armored infantry;
call up the fastest troops among our cavalry,
the mobile squadrons and the archers. We'll march

against the Bacchae! Affairs are out of hand   785
if we tamely endure such conduct in our women.

(Exit attendant to the side.)

DIONYSUS

Pentheus, you seem to hear, and yet you disregard
my words of warning. You have done me wrong,
and yet, in spite of that, I warn you once
again: do not take arms against a god.
Stay quiet here. Bromius will not let you   790
drive his women from their worship on the mountains.

PENTHEUS

Don't you lecture me. You escaped from prison.
Or shall I punish you again?

DIONYSUS

                                If I were you,
I would offer him a sacrifice, not rage
and kick against necessity, a man defying   795
god.

PENTHEUS

        I shall give your god the sacrifice
that he deserves: the blood of those same women.
I shall make a great slaughter in the woods of Cithaeron.

DIONYSUS

You will all be routed, shamefully defeated,
when their wands of ivy turn back your shields
of bronze.

PENTHEUS

                Impossible to wrestle with this foreigner!   800
Whether he's victim or culprit, he won't hold his tongue.

DIONYSUS

                        Friend,
you can still save the situation.

PENTHEUS

How?
By accepting orders from my own slaves?

DIONYSUS

No.
I undertake to lead the women back to Thebes.
Without weapons.

PENTHEUS

This is some trap.

DIONYSUS

A trap?   805
How so, if I save you by my own devices?

PENTHEUS

I know.
You and they have agreed to establish your rites
forever.

DIONYSUS

True, I've agreed to this—with the god.

PENTHEUS

Bring my armor, someone. And you—stop talking!   810

DIONYSUS

Wait!
Would you like to see them sitting on the mountains?

PENTHEUS

I would pay a lot of gold to see that sight.

DIONYSUS

What? Are you so passionately curious?

PENTHEUS

Of course
I'd be sorry to see them drunk.

DIONYSUS

But for all your pain,   815
you'd be very glad to see it?

PENTHEUS

Yes, very much.
I could crouch beneath the fir trees, quietly.

DIONYSUS

But if you try to hide, they will track you down.

PENTHEUS

Your point is well taken. I will go openly.

DIONYSUS

Shall I lead you there now? Are you ready to go?

PENTHEUS

The sooner the better. I want no delay!   820

DIONYSUS

Then you must dress yourself in women's clothes.

PENTHEUS

Why?
I'm a man. You want me to become a woman?

DIONYSUS

If they see that you're a man, they'll kill you instantly.

PENTHEUS

True. You are an old hand at cunning, I see.

DIONYSUS

Dionysus taught me everything I know.   825

PENTHEUS

How can we arrange to follow your advice?

DIONYSUS

I'll go inside with you and help you dress.

PENTHEUS

In a woman's dress, you mean? I'd be ashamed.

DIONYSUS

Then you no longer hanker to see the maenads?

PENTHEUS

What is this costume I must wear?

DIONYSUS

                    On your head   830
I shall make your hair long and luxuriant.

PENTHEUS

                    And then?

DIONYSUS

Next, robes to your feet and a headband for your hair.

PENTHEUS

Yes? Go on.

DIONYSUS

          Then a thyrsus for your hand
and a skin of dappled fawn.

PENTHEUS

                    I could not bear it.   835
I cannot bring myself to dress in women's clothes.

DIONYSUS

Then you must fight the Bacchae. That means bloodshed.

PENTHEUS

Right. First we must go and reconnoiter.

DIONYSUS

Surely a wiser course than that of hunting bad
with worse.

PENTHEUS

          But how can I pass through the city
without being seen?

DIONYSUS

We shall take deserted streets.   840
I will lead the way.

PENTHEUS

It's all fine with me,
provided those women of Bacchus don't jeer at me.
First, however, I shall ponder your advice,°
whether to go or not.

DIONYSUS

Do as you please.
I am ready, whatever you decide.

PENTHEUS

I'll go in.
Either I shall march with my army to the mountain   845
or act on your advice.

(Exit Pentheus into the palace.)

DIONYSUS

Women, our prey is walking
into the net we threw. He shall see the Bacchae
and pay the price with death.
O Dionysus,
now action rests with you. And you are near.
Punish this man. But first distract his wits;   850
bewilder him with madness. For sane of mind
this man would never wear a woman's dress;
but obsess his soul and he will not refuse.
After those threats with which he was so fierce,
I want him made the laughingstock of Thebes,
led through the town in woman's form.
But now   855
I shall go and costume Pentheus in the clothes
which he will wear to Hades when he dies, butchered
by the hands of his mother. He shall come to know

Dionysus, son of Zeus, consummate god,   860
most terrible, and yet most gentle, to humankind.

(Exit Dionysus into the palace.)

CHORUS [*singing*]
                      STROPHE
When shall I dance once more
    with bare feet the all-night dances,
    tossing my head for joy
    in the damp air, in the dew,   865
    as a running fawn would frisk
    for the green joy of the wide fields,
    freed from fear of the hunt,
    freed from the circling beaters   870
    and the nets of woven mesh
    and the hunters hallooing on
    their yelping packs? And then, hard pressed,
    she sprints with the quickness of wind,
    bounding over the marsh,
        leaping for joy by the river,   875
    joyous at the green of the leaves,
        where no man is.
What is wisdom? What gift of the gods°
    is held in honor like this:
    to hold your hand victorious
    over the heads of those you hate?   880
Honor is cherished forever.

                   ANTISTROPHE
Slow but unmistakable
    the might of the gods moves.
    It punishes that man
    who honors folly
    and with mad conceit   885
    disregards the gods.
    The gods are crafty:

they lie in ambush
a long step of time
to hunt the unholy. 890
Beyond the old beliefs,
no thought, no act shall go.
Small, small is the cost
to believe in this:
whatever is god is strong,
whatever long time has sanctioned, 895
and the law of nature.
What is wisdom? What gift of the gods°
is held in honor like this:
to hold your hand victorious
over the heads of those you hate? 900
Honor is cherished forever.

EPODE

Blessed is he who escapes a storm at sea,
who comes home to his harbor.
Blessed is he who emerges from under affliction.
In various ways one man outraces another in the
race for wealth and power. 905
Ten thousand men possess ten thousand hopes.
A few bear fruit in happiness; the others go awry.
But he who garners day by day a happy life, 910
him I call truly blessed.

(Enter Dionysus from the palace.)

DIONYSUS

Pentheus! If you are still so curious to see
and do forbidden sights, forbidden things,
come out. Let us see you in your woman's dress,
disguised in maenad clothes so you may go and spy 915
upon your mother and her company.

(Enter Pentheus from the palace, dressed as a
bacchant and carrying a thyrsus.)

                            Why,
you look exactly like one of the daughters of Cadmus.

PENTHEUS

   I seem to see two suns blazing in the heavens.
   And now two Thebes, two cities, and each
   with seven gates. And you—you are a bull   920
   who walks before me there. Horns have sprouted
   from your head. Have you always been a beast?
   Well, now you have become a bull.

DIONYSUS
                            The god
   was hostile formerly, but now declares a truce
   and goes with us. You now see what you should.

PENTHEUS   *(Coyly primping.)*
   How do I look in my getup? Don't I move like Ino?   925
   Or like my mother Agave?

DIONYSUS
                            So much alike
   I think I might be seeing one of them. But look:
   one of your curls has come loose from under the band
   where I tucked it.

PENTHEUS
                    It must have worked loose
   when I was dancing for joy and tossing my head.   930

DIONYSUS
   Then let me assist you now and tuck it back.
   Hold still.

PENTHEUS
                    Arrange it. I am in your hands
   completely.

                            (Dionysus rearranges Pentheus' hair.)

DIONYSUS

And your strap has slipped. Yes,   935
and your robe hangs askew at the ankles.

PENTHEUS   (Bending backward to look.)
                              I think so.
At least on my right leg. But on the left the hem
lies straight.

DIONYSUS

You will think me the best of friends
when you see to your surprise how chaste the Bacchae are.   940

PENTHEUS

But to be a real bacchant, should I hold
the wand in my right hand? Or this way?

DIONYSUS

No.
In your right hand. And raise it as you raise
your right foot. I commend your change of heart.

PENTHEUS

Could I lift Cithaeron up, do you think?   945
Shoulder the cliffs, Bacchae and all?

DIONYSUS

If you wanted.
Your mind was once unsound, but now you think
as sane men do.

PENTHEUS

Should we take crowbars with us?
Or should I put my shoulder to the cliffs   950
and heave them up?

DIONYSUS

What? And destroy the haunts
of the nymphs, the holy groves where Pan plays
his woodland pipes?

PENTHEUS

                        You are right. In any case,
women should not be mastered by brute strength.
I will hide myself among the firs instead.

DIONYSUS

You will find all the ambush you deserve,   955
creeping up to spy on the maenads.

PENTHEUS

                        Think.
I can see them already, there among the bushes,
mating like birds, caught in the toils of love.

DIONYSUS

Exactly. This is your mission: you go to watch.
You may surprise them—or they may surprise you.   960

PENTHEUS

Then lead me through the very heart of Thebes,
since I'm the only one who's man enough to go.

DIONYSUS

You and you alone will labor for your city.
A great ordeal awaits you, the one that you're allotted
as your fate. I shall lead you safely there;   965
someone else shall bring you back . . .

PENTHEUS

                    Yes, my mother.

DIONYSUS

. . . conspicuous to all men.

PENTHEUS

                   It is for that I go.

DIONYSUS

You will be carried home . . .

PENTHEUS

O luxury!

DIONYSUS

. . . cradled in your mother's arms.

PENTHEUS

You will spoil me!

DIONYSUS

Yes, in a certain way.

PENTHEUS

I go to my reward.   970

DIONYSUS

You are an extraordinary young man, and you go
to an extraordinary experience. You shall win
fame high as heaven.
                              Agave, Cadmus' daughters,°
reach out your hands! I bring this young man
to a great contest, where I shall be the victor,   975
I—and Bromius. The rest the event shall show.

(Exit Dionysus to the side, followed by Pentheus.)

CHORUS [*singing*]

STROPHE

Run to the mountain, fleet hounds of madness!
   Run, run to the holy company of Cadmus' daughters!
   Sting them against the man in women's clothes,   980
   the madman who spies on the maenads!
   From behind the rocks, keen-sighted,
   his mother shall see him spying first.
   She will cry to the maenads: 985
   "Who is this who has come
   to the mountains to peer at the mountain revels
   of the women of Thebes?
   Who bore him, Bacchae?

This man was born of no woman. Some lioness
    gave him birth, some Libyan Gorgon!"   990
O Justice,
    come! Be manifest; reveal yourself with a sword!
    Stab through the throat that godless, lawless, unjust man,
        the earth-born spawn of Echion!   995

ANTISTROPHE

Uncontrollable, the unbeliever goes,°
    in spitting rage, rebellious and amok,
    madly assaulting Bacchus' mysteries and his mother's.
    Against the unassailable he runs, with rage   1000
    obsessed. But death will chastise his ideas.°
    To accept the gods, to act as a mortal—
    that is a life free from pain.
    I do not resent wisdom and I rejoice to hunt it.   1005
    But other things are great and clear
    and make life beautiful:
    purity, piety, day into night,
    honoring the gods,
    rejecting customs outside justice.   1010
O Justice,
    come! Be manifest; reveal yourself with a sword!
    Stab through the throat that godless, lawless, unjust man,
    the earth-born spawn of Echion!   1015

EPODE

O Dionysus, reveal yourself a bull! Be manifest,
    a snake with darting heads, a lion breathing fire!
    O Bacchus, go! Go with your smile!
    Cast your deadly noose about this man who hunts
    your Bacchae! Make him fall   1020
        to your maenad throng!

(Enter from the side a servant of Pentheus as a second Messenger.)

MESSENGER
How prosperous in Hellas these halls once were,

this house founded by Cadmus, the old man from Sidon° 1025
who sowed the earth-born crop of the dragon snake!
I am a slave and nothing more, yet even so
I mourn the fortunes of this fallen house.°

CHORUS LEADER

What is it?
Is there news from the Bacchae?

MESSENGER

This is my news:
Pentheus, the son of Echion, is dead. 1030

CHORUS [singing and continuing to sing in the following]
All hail to Bromius! Our god is a great god!

MESSENGER

What is this you say, woman? You dare to rejoice
at these disasters which destroy this house?

CHORUS

I am no Greek. I hail my god
in barbarian song. No longer need I
shrink with fear of prison. 1035

MESSENGER

If you suppose this city is so short of men . . .°

CHORUS

Dionysus, Dionysus, not Thebes,
has power over me.

MESSENGER

Your feelings might be forgiven, then. But this,
your exultation in disaster—it is not right. 1040

CHORUS

Tell us how that lawless man died.
How was he killed?

MESSENGER
There were three of us in all: Pentheus and I,
attending my master, and that stranger who volunteered
to guide us to the show. Leaving behind us
the last outlying farms of Thebes, we forded
the Asopus and struck into the barren scrubland   1045
of Cithaeron.
            There in a grassy glen we halted,
unmoving, silent, without a word,
so we might see but not be seen. From that vantage,   1050
in a steep meadow along the sheer rock of the cliffs,
a place where water ran and the pines grew dense
with shade, we saw the maenads sitting, their hands
busily moving at their happy tasks. Some
wound the stalks of their tattered wands with tendrils   1055
of fresh ivy; others, frisking like fillies
newly freed from the painted bridles, chanted
in Bacchic songs, responsively.
            But Pentheus—
unhappy man—could not quite see the companies
of women. "Stranger," he said, "from where we stand,
I cannot see these counterfeited maenads.°   1060
But if I climbed that towering fir that overhangs
the banks, then I could see their shameless orgies
better."
            And now the stranger worked a miracle.
Reaching for the highest branch of the great fir,
he bent it down, down, down to the dark earth,   1065
till it was curved the way a taut bow bends
or like a rim of wood when forced about the circle
of a wheel. Like that he forced that mountain fir
down to the ground. No mortal could have done it.
Then he seated Pentheus at the highest tip   1070
and with his hands let the trunk rise straightly up,
slowly and gently, lest it throw its rider.
And the tree rose, towering to heaven, with my master

seated at the top. And now the maenads saw him
more clearly than he saw them. But barely had they seen,   1075
when the stranger vanished and there came a great voice
out of heaven—Dionysus', it must have been—
crying: "Women, I bring you the man who mocks
at you and me and at our holy mysteries.   1080
Take vengeance upon him." And as he spoke
a flash of awful fire bound earth and heaven.

    The high air hushed, and along the forest glen
the leaves hung still; you could hear no cry of beasts.   1085
The Bacchae heard that voice but missed its words,
and leaping up, they stared, peering everywhere.
Again that voice. And now they knew his cry,
the clear command of Bacchius. Breaking loose
like startled doves,° through grove and torrent,   1090
over rocks, the Bacchae flew, their feet maddened
by the god's breath. And when they saw my master
perching on his tree, they climbed a great rock   1095
that towered opposite his perch and showered him
with stones and branches of fir, while the others
hurled their wands. What grim target practice!
But they didn't hit Pentheus, barely out of reach   1100
of their eager hands, treed, unable to escape.
Finally they splintered branches from the oaks
and with those bars of wood tried to lever up the tree
by prying at the roots. But every effort failed.   1105
Then Agave cried out: "Maenads, make a circle
about the trunk and grip it with your hands.
Unless we take this climbing beast, he will reveal
the secrets of the god." With that, thousands of hands
tore the fir tree from the earth, and down, down   1110
from his high perch fell Pentheus, tumbling
to the ground, sobbing and screaming as he fell,
for he knew his end was near.
               His own mother,
like a priestess with her victim, fell upon him

first. But snatching from his hair the headband   1115
so poor Agave would recognize and spare him, he said,
touching her cheeks, "No, Mother! I am Pentheus,
your own son, the child you bore to Echion!
Pity me, spare me, Mother! I have done a wrong,   1120
but do not kill your own son for that offense."
But she was foaming at the mouth, and her crazed eyes
rolled with frenzy. She was mad, stark mad,
possessed by Bacchus. Ignoring his cries of pity,
she seized his left arm at the wrist; then, planting   1125
her foot upon his chest, she pulled, wrenching away
the arm at the shoulder—not by her own strength,
for the god had put inhuman power in her hands.
Ino, meanwhile, on the other side, was scratching off
his flesh. Then Autonoë and the whole horde   1130
of Bacchae swarmed upon him. Shouts everywhere—
him groaning with what little breath was left,
them shrieking in triumph. One bore off an arm,
another a foot still warm in its shoe. His ribs
were clawed clean of flesh and every hand   1135
was smeared with blood as they played ball with scraps
of Pentheus' body.

        The pitiful remains lie scattered,
one piece among the sharp rocks, others
among the leaves in the deep woods—not easy
to search for. His mother, picking up his head,   1140
impaled it on her wand. She seems to think it is
some mountain lion's head which she carries in triumph
through the thick of Cithaeron. Leaving her sisters
at the maenad dances, she is coming here, gloating
over her grisly prize. She calls upon Bacchius: 1145
he is her "fellow huntsman," "comrade of the chase,"
"crowned with victory." But all the victory
she carries home is her own grief.

        Now,
before Agave returns, I shall leave

this scene of sorrow. Humility,
a sense of reverence before the sons of heaven—   1150
of all the prizes that a mortal man might win,
these, I say, are wisest; these are best.

(*Exit Messenger to the side.*)

CHORUS [*singing*]
Let us dance to the glory of Bacchius,
    dance to the death of Pentheus,
    the death of the spawn of the dragon!   1155
    He dressed in woman's dress;
    he took the lovely thyrsus;
    it waved him down to death,°
        led by a bull to Hades.
    Hail, Bacchae of Thebes!   1160
    Your victory is fair, fair the prize,
        this famous prize of grief, of tears!
    Glorious the game, to fold your child
    in your arms, streaming with his blood!

(*Enter Agave from the side carrying the head of
Pentheus impaled upon her thyrsus.*)

CHORUS LEADER
But look: here comes Pentheus' mother, Agave,   1165
running wild-eyed toward the palace.
                    Welcome,
welcome to the reveling band of the god of joy!

AGAVE [*singing in this lyric interchange with the Chorus, who sing in
reply*]
                    STROPHE
Bacchae of Asia . . .

CHORUS
                    Tell me.

AGAVE
. . . we bring this branch to the palace,

this fresh-cut tendril from the mountains.   1170
Happy was the hunting.

CHORUS
                                        I see.
I welcome our fellow-reveler.

AGAVE
The cub of a wild mountain lion,°
and snared by me without a noose—
look, look!   1175

CHORUS
Where was he caught?

AGAVE
                                        Cithaeron . . .

CHORUS
Cithaeron?

AGAVE
                                        . . . killed him.

CHORUS
Who struck him?

AGAVE
                                The first honor is mine.
The maenads call me "Agave the blest."   1180

CHORUS
And then who?

AGAVE
                        Cadmus' . . .

CHORUS
                                Cadmus'?

AGAVE
                                . . . daughters.

After me, they hit the prey.
After me. Happy was their hunting.

ANTISTROPHE

Share the feast!

CHORUS

Share, unhappy woman?

AGAVE

See, the cub is young and tender.   1185
Beneath the soft mane of hair,
the down is blooming on the cheeks.

CHORUS

Yes, that mane does look like a wild beast's.

AGAVE

Our god is wise. Cunningly, cleverly,   1190
Bacchius the hunter lashed the maenads
against his prey.

CHORUS

Our king is a hunter.

AGAVE

Do you praise?

CHORUS

Yes, I praise.

AGAVE

The men of Thebes soon . . .

CHORUS

. . . and Pentheus, your son . . .

AGAVE

. . . will praise his mother. She caught   1195
a great quarry, this lion's cub.

CHORUS
Extraordinary catch.

AGAVE

Extraordinary skill.

CHORUS
You are proud?

AGAVE

Proud and happy.
I have won the trophy of the chase,
a great prize, manifest to all.

CHORUS LEADER [*speaking*]
Then, poor woman, show the citizens of Thebes   1200
this great prize, this trophy you have won
in the hunt.

AGAVE [*speaking*]
                    You citizens of this towered city,
men of Thebes, behold the trophy of your women's
hunting! This is the quarry of our chase, taken
not with nets nor Thessalian spears but by   1205
the dainty hands of women. What are they worth,
your javelins now and all that uselessness
your armor is, since we, with our bare hands,
captured this quarry and tore its bleeding body
limb from limb?
                    But where is my old father, Cadmus?   1210
He should come. And my son. Where is Pentheus?
Fetch him. I will have him set his ladder up
against the wall and, there upon the beam,
nail the head of this wild lion I have killed
as a trophy of my hunt.

(*Enter Cadmus from the side, with attendants bearing a covered bier.*)

CADMUS

        Follow me, attendants.   1215
Bear your dreadful burden of Pentheus and set it down
there before the palace.

                     (The attendants do as instructed.)

        Now I bring it,
this body—after long and weary searchings
I painfully gathered it from Cithaeron's glens
where it lay, scattered in shreds, dismembered
throughout the forest, no two pieces   1220
in a single place.°
        Old Teiresias and I
had returned to Thebes from the Bacchae on the mountain
before I learned of this atrocious crime
my daughters did. And so I hurried back
to the mountain to recover the body of this boy   1225
murdered by the maenads. There among the oaks
I found Aristaeus' wife, the mother of Actaeon,
Autonoë, and with her Ino, both
still stung with madness. But Agave, they said,
was on her way to Thebes, still possessed.   1230
And what they said was true, for there she is,
and not a happy sight.

AGAVE

               Now, Father,
yours can be the proudest boast of living men,
because you are the father of the bravest daughters
in the world. All of your daughters are brave,   1235
but I above the rest. I have left my shuttle
at the loom; I raised my sight to higher things—
to hunting animals with my bare hands.
              You see?
Here in my hands I hold the quarry of my chase,
a trophy for our house, to be nailed up high

upon its walls. Come Father, take it in your hands.   1240
Glory in my kill and invite your friends to share
the feast of triumph. For you are blest, Father,
by this great deed we have done.

CADMUS
                              This is a grief°
so great it knows no size. I cannot look.
This is the awful murder your hands have done.   1245
This, this is the noble victim you have slaughtered
to the gods. And to share a feast like this
you now invite all Thebes and me?
                              O gods,
how terribly I pity you and then myself.
Justly—yes, but excessively has lord Bromius,
this god of our own blood, destroyed us all,   1250
every one.

AGAVE
                    How scowling and crabbed is old age
in mortals. I hope my son takes after his mother
and wins, as she has done, the laurels of the chase
when he goes hunting with the younger men of Thebes.
But all my son can do is quarrel with god.   1255
He should be scolded, Father, and you are the one
who should scold him. Yes, someone call him here
so he can see his mother's triumph.

CADMUS
                              Enough. No more.
If you realize the horror you have done,
you shall suffer terribly. But if instead   1260
your present madness lasts until you die,
you'll not seem unhappy, but you won't be happy.

AGAVE
Why do you reproach me? Is there something wrong?

CADMUS

First raise your eyes to the heavens.

AGAVE

There.   1265

But why?

CADMUS

Does it look the same as it did before?

Or has it changed?

AGAVE

It seems—somehow—clearer,

brighter than it was before.

CADMUS

Do you still feel

the same flurry inside you?

AGAVE

The same—flurry?

No, I feel—somehow—calmer. I feel as though—   1270

my mind were somehow—changing.

CADMUS

Can you still hear me?

Can you answer clearly?

AGAVE

Yes. I have forgotten

what we said before, Father.

CADMUS

Who was your husband?

AGAVE

Echion—a man, they said, born of the dragon seed.

CADMUS

What was the name of the child you bore your husband?   1275

AGAVE

Pentheus.

CADMUS

And whose head do you hold in your hands?

AGAVE

A lion's head—or so the hunters told me.

CADMUS

Look directly at it. That's quickly done.

AGAVE

Aah! What is it? What am I holding in my hands?   1280

CADMUS

Look more closely still. Study it carefully.

AGAVE

No! O gods, I see the greatest grief there is.

CADMUS

Does it look like a lion now?

AGAVE

                              No, no. It is—
Pentheus' head—I hold.

CADMUS

                              And mourned by me   1285
before you ever knew.

AGAVE

                              But who killed him?
Why am I holding him?

CADMUS

                              O savage truth,
what a time to come!

AGAVE

For god's sake, speak.
My heart is beating with terror.

CADMUS

You killed him.
You and your sisters.

AGAVE

But where was he killed?   1290
Here at home? Where?

CADMUS

He was killed on Cithaeron,
there where the hounds tore Actaeon to pieces.

AGAVE

But why? Why had Pentheus gone to Cithaeron?

CADMUS

He went to your revels to mock the god.

AGAVE

But we—
what were we doing on the mountain?

CADMUS

You were mad.   1295
The whole city was possessed.

AGAVE

Now, now I see:
Dionysus has destroyed us all.

CADMUS

You outraged him.
You denied that he was truly god.

AGAVE

Father,
where is my poor boy's body now?

CADMUS
                    There it is.
I gathered the pieces with great difficulty.

AGAVE
Is his body entire? Has he been laid out well?   1300

CADMUS
. . . .°

AGAVE
But how did Pentheus share in my own folly?

CADMUS
He, like you, blasphemed the god. And so
the god has brought us all to ruin at one blow,
you, your sisters, and this boy. All our house
the god has utterly destroyed and, with it,
me. For I have no sons, have no male heir;   1305
and I have lived only to see this boy,
this fruit of your own body, most horribly
and foully killed.

                                        (To the corpse.)

                    To you my house looked up.
Child, you were the stay of my house; you were
my daughter's son. Of you this city stood in awe.   1310
No one who once had seen your face dared outrage
the old man, for if he did, you punished him.
Now I must go, a banished and dishonored man—
I, Cadmus the great, who sowed the soldiery
of Thebes and harvested a great harvest. My son,   1315
dearest to me of all men—for even dead,
I count you still the man I love the most—
never again will your hand touch my chin;
no more, child, will you hug me and call me
"Grandfather" and say, "Who is wronging you?   1320
Does anyone trouble you or vex your heart, old man?

Tell me, Grandfather, and I will punish him."
No, now there is grief for me; the mourning
for you; pity for your mother; and for her sisters,
sorrow.

     If there is still any mortal man   1325
who despises or defies divinity, let him look
on this boy's death and believe in the gods.

CHORUS LEADER
Cadmus, I pity you. Your daughter's son
has died as he deserved, and yet his death
bears hard on you.

AGAVE
          O Father, now you can see
how all my life has changed.
. . . .*°

DIONYSUS   *(Addressing Cadmus.)*
          You, Cadmus, shall be changed   1330
to a serpent, and your wife, the child of Ares,

---

*At this point there is a break in the manuscript of at least fifty lines. The general outlines of the missing section can be reconstructed as follows: Agave, aware that she is now polluted, asks if she may nonetheless lay her son's corpse out so that she can say farewell to him and he can be buried. Cadmus agrees but warns her of its pitiful state. Leaning over the body, she voices piteous accusations against herself, embracing Pentheus' limbs one by one and mourning over them. Suddenly Dionysus appears above the palace, probably no longer in his human disguise but in his divine splendor, and addresses all those present: He accuses the Thebans, who had denied his divinity and rejected his gift of wine, and especially Pentheus for his many outrages against him. He then foretells the future of each survivor in turn: the descendants of Cadmus will someday be banished from Thebes; Agave and her sisters must immediately be exiled as murderers. Finally the god addresses Cadmus; it is at this point that the manuscript resumes. For the sources used by scholars to reconstruct the missing section, see the textual note on line 1329; see also the introduction to this play. Arrowsmith's own hypothetical version of the missing section is provided in the appendix.

immortal Harmonia, shall undergo your doom,
a serpent too. With her, it is your fate
to make a journey in a cart drawn on by oxen,
leading behind you a huge barbarian host.
For thus decrees the oracle of Zeus.
You shall ravage many cities; but when your army   1335
plunders the shrine of Apollo, its homecoming
shall be wretched and hard. Yet in the end
the god Ares shall save Harmonia and you
and settle you both in the Land of the Blessed.
    So say I, born of no mortal father,   1340
Dionysus, true son of Zeus. If then,
when you would not, you had muzzled your madness
and been self-controlled, you'd all be happy now,
and would have the son of Zeus as your ally.

CADMUS°
We implore you, Dionysus. We have done wrong.

DIONYSUS
Too late. You did not know me when you should have.   1345

CADMUS
We have learned. But you punish us too harshly.

DIONYSUS
I am a god. I was blasphemed by you.

CADMUS
Gods should be exempt from human passions.

DIONYSUS
Long ago my father Zeus ordained these things.

AGAVE
It is fated, Father. We must go.

DIONYSUS
                Why then delay?   1350
For you must go.

(*Exit Dionysus.*)°

CADMUS

          Child, to what a dreadful end
have we all° come, poor you, your wretched sisters,
and my unhappy self. An old man, I must go
to live a stranger among barbarian peoples, doomed   1355
to lead against Hellas a motley barbarian army.
Transformed to serpents, I and my wife,
Harmonia, the child of Ares, we must captain
spearmen against the tombs and shrines of Hellas.
Never shall my sufferings end; not even   1360
in Hades shall I ever have peace.

AGAVE

                   O Father,
to be banished, to live without you!

CADMUS

                Poor child,
like a swan embracing its hoary, worn-out father,   1365
why do you clasp your arms about my neck?

AGAVE

But banished! Where shall I go?

CADMUS

                 I do not know,
my child. Your father can no longer help you.

AGAVE [*chanting*]
Farewell, my home! City, farewell.
O bedchamber, banished I go,   1370
in misery, I leave you now.

CADMUS [*chanting henceforth*]
Go, poor child, to the burial place°
of Aristaeus' son on Cithaeron.

AGAVE [*chanting*]
I pity you, Father.

CADMUS
                         And I pity you, my child,
    and I grieve for your poor sisters. I pity them.

AGAVE [singing]
    Terribly has Dionysus brought°   1375
    disaster down upon this house.

CADMUS°
    He was terribly blasphemed by us,
    his name dishonored in Thebes.

AGAVE [chanting henceforth]
    Farewell, Father.

CADMUS
                         Farewell to you, unhappy child.
    Fare well. But you shall find your faring hard.   1380

AGAVE
    Lead me, guides, to where my sisters wait,
    poor sisters of my exile. Let me go
    where I shall never see Cithaeron more,
    where that accursed hill may not see me,°   1385
    where I shall find no trace of thyrsus!
         All that I leave to other Bacchae.

       (Exit Cadmus and Agave to the side with the bier and attendants.)

CHORUS [chanting]
    The gods have many shapes.°
    The gods bring many things
    to accomplishment unhoped.
    And what was most expected   1390
    has not been accomplished.
    But god has found his way
    for what no man expected.
         So ends this story.

APPENDIX TO THE BACCHAE

This appendix provides Arrowsmith's hypothetical version of
the section missing after line 1329.

AGAVE

I am in anguish now,
tormented, who walked in triumph minutes past,
exulting in my kill. And that prize I carried home
with such pride was my own curse. Upon these hands
I bear the curse of my son's blood. How then
with these accursed hands may I touch his body?
How can I, accursed with such a curse, hold him
to my breast? O gods, what dirge can I sing
[that there might be] a dirge [for every]
broken limb?

. . . .

Where is a shroud to cover up his corpse?
O my child, what hands will give you proper care
unless with my own hands I lift my curse?

> (She lifts up one of Pentheus' limbs and asks the help of
> Cadmus in piecing the body together. She mourns each
> piece separately before replacing it on the bier.)

Come, Father. We must restore his head
to this unhappy boy. As best we can, we shall make
him whole again.
—O dearest, dearest face!
Pretty boyish mouth! Now with this veil

I shroud your head, gathering with loving care
these mangled bloody limbs, this flesh I brought
to birth

. . . .

CHORUS LEADER
Let this scene teach those [who see these things:
Dionysus is the son] of Zeus.

(Above the palace Dionysus appears in epiphany.)

DIONYSUS
[I am Dionysus,
the son of Zeus, returned to Thebes, revealed,
a god to men.] But the men [of Thebes] blasphemed me.
They slandered me; they said I came of mortal man,
and not content with speaking blasphemies,
[they dared to threaten my person with violence.]
These crimes this people whom I cherished well
did from malice to their benefactor. Therefore,
I now disclose the sufferings in store for them.
Like [enemies], they shall be driven from this city
to other lands; there, submitting to the yoke
of slavery, they shall wear out wretched lives,
captives of war, enduring much indignity.

(He turns to the corpse of Pentheus.)

This man has found the death which he deserved,
torn to pieces among the jagged rocks.
You are my witnesses: he came with outrage;
he attempted to chain my hands, abusing me
[and doing what he should least of all have done.]
And therefore he has rightly perished by the hands
of those who should the least of all have murdered him.
What he suffers, he suffers justly.
                            Upon you,
Agave, and on your sisters I pronounce this doom:

you shall leave this city in expiation
of the murder you have done. You are unclean,
and it would be a sacrilege that murderers
should remain at peace beside the graves [of those
whom they have killed].

(He turns to Cadmus.)

ALCESTIS

EURIPIDES
Translated by Richmond Lattimore

INTRODUCTION TO EURIPIDES' ALCESTIS

Alcestis, the earliest extant play of Euripides, was produced in 438 BCE and won second prize.

The given story was that Admetus, king of Thessaly, could avoid his fated death if someone else would volunteer to die in his place. Alcestis, his wife, did so; no other would. But Heracles, a long-time friend of Admetus, fought Death and took Alcestis away from him and restored her to her husband. The story had been previously dramatized by Phrynichus, the early fifth-century tragedian, in a lost play.

Euripides could have made the only point of his action the heroism of the wife. He does, of course, acknowledge and celebrate this, but the story is also the story of Admetus, the man who let his wife die in his place, his struggle with the unstated fact, and his final acknowledgment of it. This comes just before her restoration and helps us understand the miraculous favor shown him by his friends, Apollo and Heracles, as a reward for his justice and hospitality.

A tragedy with a happy ending, almost a tragedy in reverse, *Alcestis* occupied fourth place in its series and is thus a substitute for the cheerful, ribald satyr-play which customarily followed the tragic trilogy. It is probably unwise, however, to try to see any actual elements of satyr-play in it, except for the temporary drunkenness of Heracles, which, as far as it goes, is in the manner of satyr-play and comedy. Overall, the play is remarkable for its unsettling, bittersweet tone, neither purely tragic nor purely comic but a mixture of both.

ALCESTIS

Characters   APOLLO
DEATH
CHORUS of citizens of Pherae
MAID, attendant of Alcestis
ALCESTIS, wife of Admetus
ADMETUS of Pherae, king of Thessaly
BOY,° son of Admetus and Alcestis
HERACLES, friend of Admetus
PHERES, father of Admetus
SERVANT of Admetus

Scene: Pherae, in Thessaly, in front of the house of Admetus

                (Enter Apollo from the house, armed with a bow.)

APOLLO

House of Admetus, in which I, god though I am,
had patience to accept the table of the serfs!
Zeus was the cause. Zeus killed my son, Asclepius,
and drove the bolt of the hot lightning through his chest.
I, in my anger for this, killed the Cyclopes,   5
smiths of Zeus's fire, for which my father made me serve
a mortal man, in penance for what I did.
I came to this country, tended the oxen of this host
and friend, Admetus, son of Pheres, and have kept
his house from danger until this very day.   10
For I, who know what's right, have found in him
a man who knows what's right, and so I saved him

from dying, tricking the Fates. The goddesses promised me
Admetus would escape the moment of his death
by giving the lower powers someone else to die
instead of him. He tried his loved ones all in turn,   15
father and aged mother who had given him birth,°
and found not one, except his wife, who would consent
to die for him, and not see daylight any more.
She is in the house now, gathered in his arms and held
at the breaking point of life, because destiny marks   20
this for her day of death and taking leave of life.
The stain of death in the house must not be on me. I
step therefore from these chambers dearest to my love.
And here is Death himself, I see him coming, Death
who dedicates the dying, who will lead her down   25
to the house of Hades. He has come on time. He has
been watching for this day on which her death falls due.

(Enter Death from the side, armed with a sword.)

DEATH [*chanting*]
Ah!
You at this house, Phoebus? Why do you haunt
the place? It is unfair to take for your own   30
and spoil the death-spirits' privileges.
Was it not enough, then, that you blocked the death
of Admetus, and overthrew the Fates
by a shabby wrestler's trick? And now
your bow hand is armed to guard her too,   35
Alcestis, Pelias' daughter, though she
promised her life for her husband's.

APOLLO
Never fear. I have nothing but justice and fair words for you.

DEATH [*now speaking*]
If you mean fairly, what are you doing with a bow?

APOLLO
It is my custom to carry it with me all the time.   40

DEATH

It is your custom to help this house more than you ought.

APOLLO

But he is my friend, and his misfortunes trouble me.

DEATH

You mean to take her corpse, too, away from me?

APOLLO

I never took his body away from you by force.

DEATH

How is it, then, that he is above ground, not below?   45

APOLLO

He gave his wife instead, and you have come for her now.

DEATH

I have. And I shall take her down where the dead are.

APOLLO

Take her and go. I am not sure you will listen to me.

DEATH

Tell me to kill whom I must kill. Such are my orders.

APOLLO

No, only to put their death off. They must die in the end.   50

DEATH

I understand what you would say and what you want.

APOLLO

Is there any way, then, for Alcestis to grow old?

DEATH

There is not. I insist on enjoying my rights too.

APOLLO

You would not take more than one life, in any case.

DEATH

My privilege means more to me when they die young.   55

APOLLO

If she dies old, she will have a lavish burial.

DEATH

What you propose, Phoebus, is to favor the rich.

APOLLO

What is this? Have you unrecognized talents for debate?

DEATH

Those who could afford to buy a late death would buy it then.

APOLLO

I see. Are you determined not to do this favor for me?   60

DEATH

I will not do it. And you know my character.

APOLLO

I know it: hateful to mankind, loathed by the gods.

DEATH

You cannot always have your way where you should not.

APOLLO

For all your brute ferocity you shall be stopped.
The man to do it is on the way to Pheres' house   65
now, on an errand from Eurystheus, sent to steal
a team of horses from the wintry lands of Thrace.
He shall be entertained here in Admetus' house
and he shall take the woman away from you by force,
nor will you have our gratitude, but you shall still   70
be forced to do it, and to have my hate beside.

DEATH

Much talk. Talking will win you nothing. All the same,
the woman will go with me to Hades' house. I go
to her now, to dedicate her with my sword,
for all whose hair is cut in consecration   75
by this blade's edge are devoted to the gods below.

(Exit Death into the house, Apollo to the side. Enter the Chorus.)

CHORUS° [*chanting*]
    It is quiet by the palace. What does it mean?
    Why is the house of Admetus so still?
    Is there none here of his family, none
    who can tell us whether the queen is dead   80
    and therefore to be mourned? Or does Pelias'
    daughter Alcestis live still, still look
    on daylight, she who in my mind appears
    noble beyond
    all women beside in a wife's duty?   85
    [*singing individually, not as a group*]

FIRST CITIZEN

STROPHE A
    Does someone hear anything?
    a groan or a hand's stroke or outcry
    in the house, as if something were done
    and over?

SECOND CITIZEN
               No. And there is no servant stationed
    at the outer gates. O Paean,   90
    healer, might you show in light
    to still the storm of disaster.

THIRD CITIZEN
    They would not be silent if she were dead.

FOURTH CITIZEN
    No, she is gone.°

FIFTH CITIZEN
    They have not taken her yet from the house.

SIXTH CITIZEN
    So sure? I know nothing. Why are you certain?   95
    And how could Admetus have buried his wife
    with none by, and she so splendid?

SEVENTH CITIZEN

ANTISTROPHE A

Here at the gates I do not see
the lustral spring water, approved
by custom for a house of death.   100

EIGHTH CITIZEN

Nor are there cut locks of hair at the forecourts
hanging, such as the stroke of sorrow
for the dead makes. I can hear no beating
of the hands of young women.

NINTH CITIZEN

Yet this is the day appointed.   105

TENTH CITIZEN

What do you mean? Speak.

NINTH CITIZEN

On which she must pass to the world below.

ELEVENTH CITIZEN

You touch me deep, my heart, my mind.

TWELFTH CITIZEN

Yes. He who from the first has claimed to be called
a good man himself   110
must grieve when good men are afflicted.

[*all singing together*]

STROPHE B

Sailing the long sea, there is
not any shrine on earth
you could visit, not Lycia,
not the unwatered sanctuary of Ammon,   115
to redeem the life
of this unhappy woman. Her fate shows
steep and near. There is no god's hearth
I know you could reach and by sacrifice   120
avail to save.

There was only one. If the eyes
of Phoebus' son Asclepius could have
seen this light, if he could have come
and left the dark chambers,   125
the gates of Hades.
He upraised those who were stricken
down, until from Zeus' hand
the flown bolt of thunder hit him.
Where is there any hope for life   130
left for me any longer?

[now chanting]
For all has been done that can be done by our kings now,
and there on all the gods' altars
are blood sacrifices dripping in full,
but no healing comes for the evil.   135

(Enter Maid from the house.)

CHORUS LEADER
But here is a serving woman coming from the house.
The tears break from her. What will she say has taken place?
We must, of course, forgive your sorrow if something
has happened to your masters. We should like to know
whether the queen is dead or if she is still alive.   140

MAID
I could tell you that she is still alive or that she is dead.

CHORUS LEADER
How could a person both be dead and live and see?

MAID
It has felled her, and the life is breaking from her now.

CHORUS LEADER
Such a husband, to lose such a wife! I pity you.

MAID

The master does not see it and he will not see it   145
until it happens.

CHORUS LEADER

There is no hope left she will live?

MAID

None. This is the day of destiny. It is too strong.

CHORUS LEADER

Surely, he must be doing all he can for her.

MAID

All is prepared so he can bury her in style.

CHORUS LEADER

Let her be sure, at least, that as she dies, there dies   150
the noblest woman underneath the sun, by far.

MAID

Noblest? Of course the noblest, who will argue that?
What shall the wife be who surpasses her? And how
could any woman show that she loves her husband more
than herself better than by consent to die for him?   155
But all the city knows that well. You shall be told
now how she acted in the house, and be amazed
to hear. For when she understood the appointed day
was come, she bathed her white body with water drawn
from running streams, then opened the cedar chest and took   160
her clothes out, and dressed in all her finery
and stood before the shrine of Hestia, and prayed:
"Mistress, since I am going down beneath the ground,
I kneel before you in this last of all my prayers.
Take good care of my children for me. Give the boy   165
a loving wife; give the girl a noble husband;
and do not let my children die like me, who gave
them birth, untimely. Let them live a happy life

through to the end and prosper here in their own land."
Afterward she approached the altars, all that stand   170
in the house of Admetus, made her prayers, and decked
     them all
with fresh sprays torn from living myrtle. And she wept
not at all, made no outcry. The advancing doom
made no change in the color and beauty of her face.
But then, in their room, she threw herself upon the bed,   175
and there she did cry, there she spoke: "O marriage bed,
it was here that I undressed my maidenhood and gave
myself up to this husband for whose sake I die.
Good-bye. I hold no grudge. But you have been my death
and mine alone. I could not break my faith with you and him: 180
I die. Some other woman will possess you now.
She will not be better, but she might be happier."
She fell on the bed and kissed it. All the coverings
were drenched in the unchecked outpouring of her tears;
but after much crying, when all her tears were shed,   185
she rolled from the couch and walked away with eyes cast
     down,
began to leave the room, but turned and turned again
to fling herself once more upon the bed. Meanwhile
the children clung upon their mother's dress, and cried,
until she gathered them into her arms, and kissed   190
first one and then the other, as in death's farewell.
And all the servants in the house were crying now
in sorrow for their mistress. Then she gave her hand
to each, and each one took it, there was none so mean
in station that she did not stop and talk with him.   195
This is what Admetus and the house are suffering. Had
he died, he would have lost her, but in this escape
he will keep such pain; it will not ever go away.

CHORUS LEADER
Admetus surely must be grieving over this
when such a wife must be taken away from him.   200

MAID

Oh yes, he is crying. He holds his wife close in his arms,
imploring her not to forsake him. What he wants
is impossible. She is dying. The sickness fades her now.
She has gone slack, just an inert weight on the arm.
Still, though so little breath of life is left in her,   205
she wants to look once more upon the light of the sun,
since this will be the last time of all, and never again.°
She must see the sun's shining circle yet one more time.
Now I must go announce your presence. It is not
everyone who bears so much good will toward our kings   210
as to stand by ready to help in their distress.
But you have been my master's friends since long ago.

(Exit Maid into the house.)

CHORUS° [singing]

STROPHE

O Zeus, Zeus, what way out of this evil
is there, what escape from this
which is happening to our princes?
A way, any way?° Must I cut short my hair   215
for grief, put upon me the black
costume that means mourning?
We must, friends, clearly we must; yet still
let us pray to the gods. The gods
have power beyond all power elsewhere.

Paean, my lord,   220
Apollo, make some way of escape for Admetus.
Grant it, oh grant it. Once you found
rescue in him. Be now
in turn his redeemer from death.
Oppose bloodthirsty Hades.   225

ANTISTROPHE

Admetus,
O son of Pheres, what a loss

to suffer, when such a wife goes.
A man could cut his throat for this, for this
and less he could bind the noose upon his neck
and hang himself. For this is   230
not only dear, but dearest of all,
this wife you will see dead
on this day before you.

> *(Enter Alcestis carried from the house on a litter, supported*
> *by Admetus and followed by her children and servants.)*

But see, see,
she is coming out of the house and her husband is with her.
Cry out aloud, mourn, you land
of Pherae for the bravest   235
of wives fading in sickness and doomed
to the Death God of the world below.

[now chanting]
I will never again say that marriage brings
more pleasure than pain. I judge by what
I have known in the past, and by seeing now   240
what happens to our king, who is losing a wife
brave beyond all others, and must live a life
that will be no life for the rest of time.

ALCESTIS [*singing in the following interchange with Admetus, while he*
speaks in reply]
STROPHE A
Sun, and light of the day,
O turning wheel of the sky, clouds that fly.   245

ADMETUS
The sun sees you and me, two people suffering,
who never hurt the gods so they should make you die.

ALCESTIS
ANTISTROPHE A
My land, and palace arching my land,
and marriage chambers of Iolcus, my own country.

ADMETUS

Raise yourself, my Alcestis, do not leave me now.   250
I implore the gods to pity you. They have the power.

ALCESTIS

STROPHE B

I see him there at the oars of his little boat in the lake,
the ferryman of the dead,
Charon, with his hand upon the oar,
and he calls me now: "What keeps you?   255
Hurry, you hold us back." He is urging me on
in angry impatience.

ADMETUS

The crossing you speak of is a bitter one for me;
ill starred; it is unfair we should be treated so.

ALCESTIS

ANTISTROPHE B

Somebody takes me, takes me, somebody takes me,
don't you see, to the courts   260
of dead men. He frowns from under dark
brows. He has wings. It is Hades.
Let me go, what are you doing, let go.
                                    Such is the road
most wretched I have to walk.

ADMETUS

Sorrow for all who love you, most of all for me
and for the children. All of us share in this grief.   265

ALCESTIS

EPODE

Let me go now, let me down,
flat. I have no strength to stand.
Hades is close to me.
The darkness creeps over my eyes. O children,
my children, you have no mother now,   270

not any longer. Daylight is yours, my children.
Look on it and be happy.

ADMETUS [*now chanting*]
Ah, a bitter word for me to hear,
heavier than any death for me.
Please by the gods, do not be so harsh   275
as to leave me, please, by your children forlorn.
No, up, and fight it.
There would be nothing left of me if you died.
All rests in you, our life, our not
having life. Your love is what we hold sacred.

ALCESTIS [*speaking*]
Admetus, you can see how it is with me. Therefore,   280
I wish to have some words with you before I die.
I put you first, and at the price of my own life
made certain you would live and see the daylight. So
I die, who did not have to die, because of you.
I could have taken any man in Thessaly   285
I wished and lived in queenly state here in this house.
But since I did not wish to live bereft of you
and with our children fatherless, I did not spare
my youth, although I had so much to live for. Yet
your father, and the mother who bore you, betrayed you,   290
though they had reached an age when it was good to die
and good to save their son and end it honorably.
You were their only one, and they had no more hope
of having other children if you died. That way
I would be living and you would live the rest of our time,   295
and you would not be alone and mourning for your wife
and tending motherless children. No, but it must be
that some god has so wrought that things shall be this way.
So be it. But swear now to do, in recompense,
what I shall ask you—not enough, oh, never enough,   300
since nothing is enough to make up for a life,
but fair, and you yourself will say so, since you love

these children as much as I do; or at least you should.
Keep them as masters in my house, and do not marry
again and give our children a stepmother   305
who will not be so kind as I, who will be jealous
and raise her hand to your children and mine. Oh no,
do not do that, do not. That is my charge to you.
For the new-come stepmother hates the children born
to a first wife; no viper could be deadlier.   310
The little boy has his father for a tower of strength.°
But you, my darling, what will your girlhood be like,
how will your father's new wife like you? She must not
make shameful stories up about you, and contrive   315
to spoil your chance of marriage in the blush of youth.
Indeed, your mother will not be there to help you
when you are married, not be there to give you strength
when your babies are born, when only a mother's help will do.
For I must die. It will not be tomorrow, not   320
the next day, or this month, the horrible thing will come,
but now, at once, I shall be counted among the dead.
Good-bye, be happy, both of you. And you, my husband,
can boast the bride you took made you the bravest wife,
and you, children, can say, too, that your mother was brave.   325

CHORUS LEADER
Fear nothing; for I dare to speak for him. He will
do all you ask. If he does not, it's his mistake.

ADMETUS
It shall be so, it shall be, do not fear, since you
were mine in life, you still shall be my bride in death
and you alone, no other girl in Thessaly   330
shall ever be called wife of Admetus in your place.
There is none so marked out in pride of father's birth
nor other form of beauty's brilliant gleam. I have
these children, they are enough; I only pray the gods
grant me the bliss to keep them as we could not keep you.   335
I shall go into mourning for you, not for just

a year, but all my life while it still lasts, my dear,
and hate the woman who gave me birth always, detest
my father. These were called my own dear ones. They were not.
You gave what was your own and dear to buy my life   340
and saved me. Am I not to lead a mourning life
when I have lost a wife like you? I shall make an end
of revelry and entertainment in my house,
the flowers and the music that here once held sway.
No, I shall never touch the lute strings ever again   345
nor have the heart to play music upon the pipe
of Libya, for you took my joy in life with you.
The skillful hands of craftsmen shall be set to work
making me an image of you to set in my room;
I'll pay my devotions to it, hold it in my arms   350
and speak your name, and clasp it close against my heart,
and think I hold my wife again, though I do not,
cold consolation, I know it, and yet even so
I might drain the weight of sorrow. You would come
to see me in my dreams and comfort me. For they   355
who love find a time's sweetness in the visions of night.
Had I the lips of Orpheus and his melody
to charm the maiden Daughter of Demeter and
her lord, and by my singing win you back from death,
I would have gone beneath the earth: not Pluto's hound   360
Cerberus could have stayed me, not the ferryman
of ghosts, Charon at his oar. I would have brought you back
to life. Wait for me, then, in that place, till I die,
and make ready the room where you will live with me,
for I shall have them bury me in the same chest   365
as you, and lay me at your side, so that my heart
shall be against your heart, and never, even in death
shall I go from you. You alone were true to me.

CHORUS LEADER
    And I, because I am your friend and you
    are mine, shall help you bear this sorrow, as I should.   370

ALCESTIS

Children, you now have heard your father promise me
that he will never marry again and not inflict
a new wife on you, but will honor my memory.

ADMETUS

I promise again. I will keep my promise to the end.

ALCESTIS

On this condition, take the children. They are yours.   375

ADMETUS

I take them, a dear gift from a dear hand.

ALCESTIS

                                    And now
you must be our children's mother, too, instead of me.

ADMETUS

I must be such, since they will no longer have you.

ALCESTIS

O children, this was my time to live, and I must go.

ADMETUS

Ah me, what shall I do without you all alone?   380

ALCESTIS

Time will soften this. The dead count for nothing at all.

ADMETUS

Oh, take me with you, for god's love, take me down there too.

ALCESTIS

No, I am dying in your place. That is enough.

ADMETUS

O god, what a wife you are taking away from me!

ALCESTIS

It is true. My eyes darken and the heaviness comes.   385

ADMETUS
But I am lost, dear, if you leave me.

ALCESTIS
There is no use
in talking to me any more. I am not there.

ADMETUS
No, lift your head up, do not leave your children thus.

ALCESTIS
I do not want to, but it is good-bye, children.

ADMETUS
Look at them—oh, look at them!

ALCESTIS
No. There is nothing more.   390

ADMETUS
Are you really leaving us?

ALCESTIS
Good-bye.

ADMETUS
Oh, I am lost.

CHORUS LEADER
It is over now. Admetus' wife is gone from us.

BOY° [singing]
STROPHE
O wicked fortune. Mother has gone down there,
father; she is not here with us
in the sunshine any more.   395
Poor mother, she went away
and left me to live all alone.
Look at her eyes, look at her hands, so still.
Hear me, mother, listen to me, oh please,   400

listen, it is I, mother,
I your little one lean and kiss
your lips, and cry out to you.

ADMETUS

She does not see, she does not hear you. You two and I
all have a hard and heavy load to carry now.   405

BOY

ANTISTROPHE

Father, I am too small to be left alone
by the mother I loved so much. Oh,
it is hard for me to bear
all this that is happening,
and you, little sister, suffer   410
with me too.° Oh, father,
your marriage was useless, useless; she did not live
to grow old with you.
She died too soon. Mother, with you gone away,
the whole house is ruined.   415

(Exit Alcestis carried into the house, followed by children and servants.)

CHORUS LEADER

Admetus, you must stand up to misfortune now.
You are not the first, and not the last of humankind
to lose a good wife. Therefore, you must understand
death is an obligation claimed from all of us.

ADMETUS

I understand it. And this evil which has struck   420
was no surprise. I knew about it long ago,
and knowledge was hard. But now, since we must bury our
    dead,
stay with me and stand by me, chant in response the hymn
to the god below who never receives libations.
To all Thessalians over whom my rule extends   425
I ordain a public mourning for my wife, to be

observed with shaving of the head and with black robes.
The horses that you drive in chariots and those
you ride single shall have their manes cut short with steel,
and there shall be no sound of pipes within the city,   430
no sound of lyres, until twelve moons have filled and gone;
for I shall never bury any dearer dead
than she, nor any who was better to me. She deserves
my thanks. She died for me, which no one else would do.

(Exit into the house.)

CHORUS [*singing*]

STROPHE A

O daughter of Pelias   435
my wish for you is a happy life
in the sunless chambers of Hades.
Now let the dark-haired lord of Death himself, and the old man,
who sits at the steering oar   440
and ferries the corpses,
know that you are the bravest of wives, by far,
ever conveyed across the lake
of Acheron in the rowboat.

ANTISTROPHE A

Much shall be sung of you   445
by the men of music to the seven-strung mountain
lyre-shell, and in poems that have no music,
in Sparta when the season turns and the month Carneian
comes back, and the moon
rides all the night;   450
in Athens also, the shining and rich.
Such is the theme of song you left
in death, for the poets.

STROPHE B

Oh, that it were in my power   455
and that I had strength to bring you
back to light from the dark of death°

with oars on the sunken river.
For you, O dearest among women, only you   460
had the hard courage
to give your life for your husband's and save
him from death. May the dust lie light
upon you, my lady. And should he now take
a new wife to his bed, he will win my horror and hatred,
mine, and your children's hatred too.   465

ANTISTROPHE B

His mother would not endure
to have her body hidden in the ground
for him, nor the aged father.°
He was theirs, but they had not courage to save him.
Oh shame, for the gray was upon them.   470
But you, in the pride
of youth, died for him and left the daylight.
May it only be mine to win
such wedded love as hers from a wife; for this
is given seldom to mortals; but were my wife such, I would have her
with me unhurt through my lifetime.   475

(Enter Heracles from the side.)

HERACLES

My friends, people of Pherae and the villages
hereby, tell me, shall I find Admetus at home?

CHORUS LEADER

Yes, Heracles, the son of Pheres is in the house.
But tell us, what is the errand that brings you here
to the land of Thessaly and this city of Pherae?   480

HERACLES

I have some work to do for Eurystheus
of Tiryns.

CHORUS LEADER

Where does it take you? On what far journey?

HERACLES

To Thrace, to take home Diomedes' chariot.

CHORUS LEADER

How can you? Do you know the man you are to meet?

HERACLES

No. I have never been where the Bistones live.   485

CHORUS LEADER

You cannot master his horses. Not without a fight.

HERACLES

It is my work, and I cannot refuse.

CHORUS LEADER

                              You must
kill him before you come back; or be killed and stay.

HERACLES

If I must fight, it will not be for the first time.

CHORUS LEADER

What good will it do you if you overpower their master?   490

HERACLES

I will take the horses home to Tiryns and its king.

CHORUS LEADER

It is not easy to put a bridle on their jaws.

HERACLES

Easy enough, unless their nostrils are snorting fire.

CHORUS LEADER

Not that, but they have teeth that tear a man apart.

HERACLES

Oh no! Mountain beasts, not horses, feed like that.   495

CHORUS LEADER

But you can see their mangers. They are caked with blood.

HERACLES

And the man who raises them? Whose son does he claim
to be?

CHORUS LEADER

Ares'. And he is lord of the golden shield of Thrace.

HERACLES

It sounds like my life and the kind of work I do.
It is a hard and steep way always that I go,   500
having to fight one after another all the sons
the war god ever got him, with Lycaon first,
again with Cycnus, and now here is a third fight
that I must have with the master of these horses. So—
I am Alcmene's son, and the man does not live   505
who will see me break before my enemy's attack.

CHORUS LEADER

Here is the monarch of our country coming
from the house himself, Admetus.

(Enter Admetus from the house.)

ADMETUS

Welcome and happiness
to you, O scion of Perseus' blood and child of Zeus.

HERACLES

Happiness to you likewise, lord of Thessaly,   510
Admetus.

ADMETUS

I could wish it. I know you mean well.

HERACLES

What is the matter? Why is there mourning and cut hair?

ADMETUS

There is one dead here whom I must bury today.

HERACLES

Not one of your children! I pray some god shield them from
that.

ADMETUS

Not they. My children are well and living in their house.   515

HERACLES

If it is your father who is gone, his time was ripe.

ADMETUS

No, he is still there, Heracles. My mother, too.

HERACLES

Surely you have not lost your wife, Alcestis.

ADMETUS

                                                    Yes
and no. There are two ways that I could answer that.

HERACLES

Did you say that she is dead or that she is still alive?   520

ADMETUS

She is, and she is no longer. It pains me.

HERACLES

I still do not know what you mean. You are being obscure.

ADMETUS

You know about her and what must happen, do you not?

HERACLES

I know that she has undertaken to die for you.

ADMETUS

How can she still be alive, then, when she has promised that?   525

HERACLES

Ah, do not mourn her before she dies. Wait for the time.

ADMETUS

The point of death is death, and the dead are lost and gone.

HERACLES

Being and nonbeing are considered different things.

ADMETUS

That is your opinion, Heracles. It is not mine.

HERACLES

Well, but whose is the mourning now? Is it in the family?   530

ADMETUS

A woman. We were speaking of a woman, were we not?

HERACLES

Was she a blood relative or someone from outside?

ADMETUS

No relation by blood, but she meant much to us.

HERACLES

How does it happen that she died here in your house?

ADMETUS

She lost her father and came here to live with us.   535

HERACLES

I am sorry,
Admetus. I wish I had found you in a happier state.

ADMETUS

Why do you say that? What do you mean to do?

HERACLES

I mean
to go on, and stay with another of my friends.

ADMETUS

No, my lord, no. The evil must not come to that.

HERACLES

The friend who stays with friends in mourning is in the way.   540

ADMETUS

The dead are dead. Go on in.

HERACLES

No. It is always wrong
for guests to revel in a house where others mourn.

ADMETUS

There are separate guest chambers. We will take you there.

HERACLES

Let me go, and I will thank you a thousand times.

ADMETUS

You shall not go to stay with any other man.   545
You there: open the guest rooms which are across the court
from the house, and tell the people who are there to provide
plenty to eat, and make sure that you close the doors
facing the inside court. It is not right for guests
to have their pleasures interrupted by sounds of grief.   550

(Heracles is escorted into the house.)

CHORUS LEADER

Admetus, are you crazy? What are you thinking of
to entertain guests in a situation like this?

ADMETUS

And if I had driven from my city and my house
the guest and friend who came to me, would you have
approved
of me more? Wrong. My misery would still have been   555
as great, and I should be inhospitable too,
and there would be one more misfortune added to those
I have, if my house is called unfriendly to its friends.
For this man is my best friend, and he is my host
whenever I go to Argos, which is a thirsty place.   560

CHORUS LEADER

Yes, but then why did you hide what is happening here
if this visitor is, as you say, your best friend?

ADMETUS

He would not have been willing to come inside my house
if he had known what trouble I was in. I know.
There are some will think I show no sense in doing this.   565
They will not like it. But my house does not know how
to push its friends away and not treat them as it should.

(Exit into the house.)

CHORUS [*singing*]

STROPHE A

O liberal and forever free-handed house of this man,
the Pythian himself, lyric Apollo,   570
was pleased to live with you
and had patience upon your lands
to work as a shepherd,
and on the hill-folds and the slopes   575
piped to the pasturing of your flocks
in their season of mating.

ANTISTROPHE A

And even dappled lynxes for delight in his melody
joined him as shepherds. From the cleft of Othrys descended   580
a red troop of lions,
and there, Phoebus, to your lyre's strain
there danced the bright-coated
fawn, adventuring from the deep   585
bearded pines, light-footed for joy
in your song, in its kindness.

STROPHE B

Therefore, your house is beyond
all others for wealth of flocks by the sweet waters
of Lake Boebias. For spread of cornland   590

and pasturing range its boundary stands
only there where the sun
stalls his horses in dark air by the Molossians.
Eastward he sways all to the harborless   595
Pelian coast on the Aegean main.

ANTISTROPHE B

Now he has spread wide his doors
and taken the guest in, when his eyes were wet
and he wept still for a beloved wife who died
in the house so lately. The noble strain   600
comes out, in respect for others.
All is there in the noble. I stand
in awe at his wisdom,° and good hope has come again to my heart
that for this godly man the end will be good.   605

(Enter Admetus from the house, followed by
servants with a covered litter.)

ADMETUS

Gentlemen of Pherae, I am grateful for your company.
My men are bearing to the burning place and grave
our dead, who now has all the state which is her due.
Will you then, as the custom is among us, say
farewell to the dead as she goes forth for the last time?   610

CHORUS LEADER

Yes, but I see your father coming now. He walks
as old men do, and followers carry in their hands
gifts for your wife, to adorn her in the underworld.

(Enter Pheres from the side.)

PHERES

I have come to bear your sorrows with you, son. I know,
nobody will dispute it, you have lost a wife   615
both good and modest in her ways. Nevertheless,
you have to bear it, even though it is hard to bear.
Accept these gifts to deck her body, bury them

with her. Oh yes, she well deserves honor in death.
She died to save your life, my son. She would not let   620
me be a childless old man, would not let me waste
away in sorrowful age deprived of you. Thereby,
daring this generous action, she has made the life
of all women become a thing of better repute
than it was.

          O you who saved him, you who raised us up   625
when we were fallen, farewell, even in Hades' house
may good befall you.

              I say people ought to marry women
like this. Otherwise, better not to marry at all.

ADMETUS

I never invited you to come and see her buried,
nor do I count your company as that of a friend.   630
She shall not wear anything that you bring her.
She needs nothing from you to be buried in. Your time
to share my sorrow was when I was about to die.
But you stood out of the way and let youth take my place
in death, though you were old. Will you cry for her now?   635
It cannot be that my body ever came from you,
nor did the woman who claims she bore me and is called
my mother give me birth. I was got from some slave
and surreptitiously put to your wife to nurse.
You show it. Your nature in the crisis has come out.   640
I do not count myself as any child of yours.
Oh, you outpass the cowardice of all the world,
you at your age, come to the very last step of life
and would not, dared not, die for your own child. Oh no,
you let this woman, married into our family,   645
do it instead, and therefore it is right for me
to call her all the father and mother that I have.
And yet you two should honorably have striven for
the right of dying for your child. The time of life
you had left for your living was short, in any case,   650

and she and I would still be living out our time°
and I should not be hurt and grieving over her.
And yet, all that a man could have to bless his life
you have had. You had your youth in kingship. There was I
your son, ready to take it over, keep your house   655
in order, so you had no childless death to fear,
with the house left to be torn apart by other claims.
You cannot justify your leaving me to death
on grounds that I disrespected your old age. Always I
showed all consideration. See what thanks I get   660
from you and from the woman who gave me birth. Go on,
get you other children—you cannot do it too soon—
who will look after your old age, and lay you out
when you are dead, and see you buried properly.
I will not do it. This hand will never bury you.   665
I am dead as far as you are concerned, and if, because
I found another savior, I still look on the sun,
I count myself that person's child and fond support.
It is meaningless, the way the old men pray for death
and complain of age and the long time they have to live.   670
Let death only come close, not one of them still wants
to die. Their age is not a burden any more.

CHORUS LEADER
Stop, stop. We have trouble enough already, child.
You will exasperate your father with this talk.

PHERES
Big words, son. Who do you think you are cursing out   675
like this? Some Lydian slave, some Phrygian that you bought?
I am a free Thessalian noble, nobly born
from a Thessalian. Are you forgetting that? You go
too far with your high-handedness. You volley brash
words at me, and fail to hit me, and then run away.   680
I gave you life, and made you master of my house,
and raised you. I am not obliged to die for you.
I do not acknowledge any tradition among us

that fathers should die for their sons. That is not Greek either.
Your natural right is to find your own happiness   685
or unhappiness. All you deserve from me, you have.
You are lord of many. I have wide estates of land
to leave you, just as my father left them to me.
What harm have I done you then? What am I taking away
from you? Do not die for me, I will not die for you.   690
You like the sunlight. Don't you think your father does?
I count the time I have to spend down there as long,
and the time to live is little, but that little is sweet.
You fought shamelessly for a way to escape death,
and passed your proper moment, and are still alive   695
because you killed her. Then, you wretch, you dare to call
me coward, when you let your woman outdare you,
and die for her magnificent young man? I see.
You have found a clever scheme by which you *never* will die.
You will always persuade the wife you have at the time   700
to die for you instead. And you, so low, then dare
blame your own people for not wanting to do this.
Silence. I tell you, as you cherish your own life,
all other people cherish theirs. And if you call
us names, you will be called names, and the names are true.   705

CHORUS LEADER
Too much evil has been said in this speech and in
that spoken before. Old sir, stop cursing your own son.

ADMETUS
No, speak, as I have spoken.° If it hurts to hear
the truth, you should not have made a mistake with me.

PHERES
I should have made a mistake if I had died for you.   710

ADMETUS
Is it the same thing to die old and to die young?

PHERES

Yes. We have only one life and not two to live.

ADMETUS

I think you would like to live a longer time than Zeus.

PHERES

Cursing your parents, when they have done you no wrong?

ADMETUS

Yes, for I found you much in love with a long life.   715

PHERES

Who is it you are burying? Did not someone die?

ADMETUS

And that she died, you foul wretch, proves your cowardice.

PHERES

You cannot say that we were involved in her death.

ADMETUS

Ah.
I hope that some day you will stand in need of me.   720

PHERES

Go on, and court more women, so they all can die.

ADMETUS

Your fault. You were not willing to die.

PHERES

                                No, I was not.
It is a sweet thing, this god's sunshine, sweet to see.

ADMETUS

That is an abject spirit, not a man's.

PHERES

                                You shall
not mock an old man while you carry out your dead.

ADMETUS

You will die in evil memory, when you do die.   725

PHERES

I do not care what they say of me when I am dead.

ADMETUS

How old age loses all the sense of shame.

PHERES

She was
not shameless, the woman you found; she was only stupid.

ADMETUS

Get out of here now and let me bury my dead.

PHERES

I'll go. You murdered her, and you can bury her.   730
But you will have her brothers still to face. You'll pay,
for Acastus is no longer counted as a man
unless he sees you punished for his sister's blood.

ADMETUS

Go and be damned, you and that woman who lives with you.
Grow old as you deserve, childless, although your son   735
still lives. You shall not come again under the same roof
with me. And if I had to proclaim by heralds that I
disown my father's house, I should have so proclaimed.

(Exit Pheres to the side.)

Now we, for we must bear the sorrow that is ours,
shall go, and lay her body on the burning place.   740

CHORUS [chanting]

Ah, cruel the price of your daring,
O generous one, O noble and brave,
farewell. May Hermes of the world below
and Hades welcome you. And if, even there,
the good fare best, may you have high honor   745
and sit by the bride of Hades.

(Exit all to the side. The stage is empty. Enter a Servant from the house.)

SERVANT

   I have known all sorts of foreigners who have come in
   from all over the world here to Admetus' house,
   and I have served them dinner, but I never yet
   have had a guest as bad as this to entertain.   750
   In the first place, he could see the master was in mourning,
   but inconsiderately came in anyway.
   Then, he refused to understand the situation
   and be content with anything we could provide,
   but when we failed to bring him something, demanded it,   755
   and took a cup with ivy on it in both hands
   and drank the wine of our dark mother, straight, until
   the flame of the wine went all through him, and heated him,
   and then he wreathed branches of myrtle on his head
   and howled, off-key. There were two kinds of music now   760
   to hear, for while he sang and never gave a thought
   to the sorrows of Admetus' house, we servants were
      mourning
   our mistress; but we could not show before our guest
   with our eyes wet. Admetus had forbidden that.
   So now I have to entertain this guest inside,   765
   this ruffian thief, this highwayman, whoever he is,
   while she is gone away from the house, and I could not
   say good-bye, stretch my hand out to her in my grief
   for a mistress who was like a mother to all the house
   and me. She gentled her husband's rages, saved us all   770
   from trouble after trouble. Am I not then right
   to hate this guest who has come here in our miseries?

(Enter Heracles from the house, drunk.)

HERACLES

   You there, with the sad and melancholy face, what is
   the matter with you? The servant who looks after guests
   should be polite and cheerful and not scowl at them.   775

But look at you. Here comes your master's dearest friend
to visit you, and you receive him with black looks
and frowns, all because of trouble in someone else's family.
Come here, I'll tell you something that will make you wiser.
Do you really know what life is like, the way it is?   780
I don't think so. How could you? Well then, listen to me.
Death is an obligation that we all must pay.
There is not one man living who can truly say
if he will be alive or dead on the next day.
Fortune is dark; she moves, but we cannot see the way   785
nor can we pin her down by expertise and study her.
There, I have told you. Now you can understand. Go on,
enjoy yourself, drink, call the life you live today
your own, but only that; the rest belongs to chance.
Then, beyond all gods, pay your best attentions to   790
Cypris, man's sweetest. There's a god who's kind.
Let everything else go and do as I prescribe
for you, that is, if I seem to talk sense. Do I?
I think so. Well, then, get rid of this too-much grief,
put flowers on your head and drink with us, fight down   795
these present troubles;° later, I know very well
that the wine splashing in the bowl will shake you loose
from these scowl-faced looks and the tension in your mind.
We are only human. Our thoughts should be human too,
since, for these solemn people and these people who scowl,   800
the whole parcel of them, if I am any judge,
life is not really life but a catastrophe.

SERVANT

I know all that. But we have troubles on our hands
now that make revelry and laughter out of place.

HERACLES

The dead woman is out of the family. Do not mourn   805
too hard. Your master and mistress are still alive.

SERVANT

What do you mean, alive? Don't you know what happened
to us?

HERACLES

Certainly, unless your master has lied to me.

SERVANT

He is too hospitable, too much.

HERACLES

Should I not then
have enjoyed myself, because some outside woman was dead?   810

SERVANT

She was an outsider indeed. That is too true.

HERACLES

Has something happened that he did not tell me about?

SERVANT

Never mind. Go. Our masters' sorrows are our own.

HERACLES

These can be no outsiders' troubles.

SERVANT

If they were,
I should not have minded seeing you enjoy yourself.   815

HERACLES

Have I been scandalously misled by my own friends?

SERVANT

You came here when we were not prepared to take in guests.
You see, we are in mourning. You can see our robes°
of black, and how our hair is cut short.

HERACLES

Who is dead?
The aged father? Or is one of the children gone?   820

SERVANT

My lord, Admetus' wife is dead.

HERACLES

What are you saying?
And all this time you were making me comfortable?

SERVANT

He was embarrassed to turn you from this house of his.

HERACLES

My poor Admetus, what a helpmeet you have lost!

SERVANT

We are all dead and done for now, not only she.   825

HERACLES

I really knew it when I saw the tears in his eyes,
his shorn hair and his face; but he persuaded me
with talk of burying someone who was not by blood
related. So, unwillingly, I came inside
and drank here in the house of this hospitable man   830
when he was in this trouble! Worse, I wreathed my head
with garlands, and drank freely. But you might have said
something about this great disaster in the house.
Now, where shall I find her? Where is the funeral being held?

SERVANT

Go straight along the Larisa road, and when you clear   835
the city you will see the monument and the mound.

(Exit the Servant into the house.)

HERACLES

O heart of mine and hand of mine, who have endured
so much already, prove what kind of son it was
Alcmene, daughter of Electryon, bore to Zeus
in Tiryns. I must save this woman who has died   840
so lately, bring Alcestis back to live in this house,
and pay Admetus all the kindness that I owe.

I must go there and watch for Death of the black robes,
master of dead men, and I think I shall find him
drinking the blood of slaughtered beasts beside the grave.   845
Then, if I can break suddenly from my hiding place,
catch him, and hold him in the circle of these arms,
there is no one who will be able to break my hold
on his bruised ribs, until he gives the woman up
to me. But if I miss my quarry, if he does not come   850
to the bloody offering, I will go down, I will ask
the Maiden and the Master in the sunless homes
of those below; and I have confidence I shall bring
Alcestis back up, and give her to the arms of my friend
who did not drive me off but took me into his house   855
and, though he staggered under the stroke of circumstance,
hid it, for he was noble and respected me.
Who in all Thessaly is a truer friend than this?
Who in all Greece? Therefore, he must not ever say
that, being noble, he befriended a worthless man.   860

(Exit Heracles to the side. Then enter Admetus from
the side, accompanied by the Chorus.)

ADMETUS [chanting]
Hateful is this
return, hateful the sight of this house
widowed, empty. Where shall I go?
Where shall I stay? What shall I say?
How can I die?
My mother bore me to a heavy fate.   865
I envy the dead. I long for those
who are gone, to live in their houses, with them.
There is no pleasure in the sunshine
nor the feel of the hard earth under my feet.
Such was the hostage Death has taken   870
from me, and given to Hades.

(While the Chorus sings, Admetus moans inarticulately.)

CHORUS

Go on, go on. Plunge in the deep of the house.
What you have suffered is enough for tears.
You have gone through pain, I know,
but you do no good to the woman who lies   875
below. Never again to look on the face
of the wife you loved hurts you.

ADMETUS [now chanting]

You have opened the wound torn in my heart.
What can be worse for a man than to lose
a faithful wife. I envy those   880
without wives, without children. I wish I had not
ever married her, lived with her in this house.
We have each one life. To grieve for this
is burden enough.
When we could live single all our days   885
without children, it is not to be endured
to see children sicken or married love
despoiled by death.

(As before: while the Chorus sings, Admetus moans inarticulately.)

CHORUS

ANTISTROPHE A

Chance comes. It is hard to wrestle against it.
There is no limit to set on your pain.   890
The weight is heavy. Yet still
bear up. You are not the first man to lose
his wife. Disaster appears, to crush
one man now, but afterward another.

ADMETUS [chanting]

How long my sorrows, the pain for my loves   895
down under the earth.
Why did you stop me from throwing myself

in the hollow cut of the grave, there to lie
dead beside her, who was best on earth?
Then Hades would have held fast two lives,   900
not one, and the truest of all, who crossed
the lake of the dead together.

CHORUS [*singing*]

STROPHE B

There was a man
of my people, who lost a boy
in his house anyone would mourn for,   905
the only child. But still
he bore the evil well enough, though childless,
and he stricken with age
and the hair gray on him,
well on in his lifetime.   910

ADMETUS [*chanting*]

O builded house, how shall I enter you?
How dwell in you, with this new turn
of my fortune? How different now and then.
Then it was with Pelian pine torches,   915
with marriage songs, that I entered my house,
with the hand of a sweet bride on my arm,
with loud rout of revelers following
to bless her who now is dead, and me,
for our high birth, for nobilities   920
from either side which were joined in us.
Now the bridal chorus has changed for a dirge,
and for white robes the costumed black
goes with me inside
to where our room stands deserted.   925

CHORUS [*singing*]

ANTISTROPHE B

Your luck had been
good, so you were inexperienced when

this grief came. Still you saved
your own life and being.
Your wife is dead, your love forsaken.   930
What is new in this? Before
now death has parted
many from their wives.

ADMETUS [*now speaking*]
   Friends, I believe my wife is happier than I   935
although I know she does not seem to be. For her,
there will be no more pain to touch her ever again.
She has her glory and is free from much distress.
But I, who should not be alive, who have passed by
my moment, shall lead a sorry life. I see it now.   940
How can I bear to go inside this house again?
Whom shall I speak to? Who will speak to me, to give
me any pleasure in coming home? Where shall I turn?
The desolation in my house will drive me out
when I see my wife's bed empty, when I see the chairs   945
she used to sit in, and all about the house the floor
unwashed and dirty, while the children at my knees
huddle and cry for their mother and the servants mourn
their mistress and remember what the house has lost.
So it will be at home, but if I go outside   950
meeting my married friends in Thessaly, the sight
of their wives will drive me back, for I cannot endure
to look at my wife's age-mates and the friends of her youth.
And anyone who hates me will say this of me:
"Look at the man, disgracefully alive, who dared   955
not die, but like a coward gave his wife instead
and so escaped death. Do you call him a man at all?
He turns on his own parents, but he would not die
himself." Besides my other troubles, they will speak
about me thus. What have I gained by living, friends,   960
when reputation, life, and action all are bad?

CHORUS [*singing*]

I myself, in the transports
of mystic verses, as in study
of history and science, have found
nothing so strong as Compulsion,   965
nor any means to combat her,
not in the Thracian books set down
in verse by the voice of Orpheus,
not in all the remedies Phoebus has given the heirs   970
of Asclepius to fight the many afflictions of man.

ANTISTROPHE A

She alone is a goddess
without altar or statue to pray
before. She heeds no sacrifice.   975
Majesty, bear no harder
on me than you have in my life before!
All Zeus himself ordains
only with you is accomplished.
By strength you fold and crumple the steel of the Chalybes.   980
There is no pity in the sheer barrier of your will.

STROPHE B

Now the goddess has caught you in the breakless grip of her hands.
Bear up. You will never bring back up, by crying,   985
the dead into the light again.
Even the sons of the gods fade
and go in death's shadow.   990
She was loved when she was with us.
She shall be loved still, now she is dead.
It was the best of all women to whom you were joined in marriage.

ANTISTROPHE B

The monument of your wife must not be counted among the graves   995
of the dead, but it must be given honors

like the gods' worship of wayfarers.
And as they turn the bend of the road   1000
and see it, men shall say:
"She died for the sake of her husband.
Now she is a blessed spirit.
Hail, majesty, be gracious to us." Thus will men speak in her
    presence.   1005

CHORUS LEADER

But here is someone who looks like Alcmene's son,
Admetus. He seems on his way to visit you.

(Enter Heracles from the side, leading a veiled woman.)

HERACLES

A man, Admetus, should be allowed to speak freely
to a friend, instead of keeping his complaints suppressed
inside him. Now, I thought I had the right to stand   1010
beside you and endure what you endured, so prove
my friendship. But you never told me that she, who lay
dead, was your wife, but entertained me in your house
as if your mourning were for some outsider's death.
And so I wreathed my head and poured libations out   1015
to the gods, in your house, though your house had
    suffered so.
This was wrong, wrong I tell you, to have treated me
thus, though I have no wish to hurt you in your grief.
Now, as for the matter of why I have come back again,
I will tell you. Take this woman, keep her safe for me,   1020
until I have killed the master of the Bistones
and come back, bringing with me the horses of Thrace.
If I have bad luck—I hope not, I hope to come
back home—I give her to the service of your house.
It cost a struggle for her to come into my hands.   1025
You see, I came on people who were holding games
for all comers, with prizes which an athlete might
well spend an effort winning.

(Points to the woman.)

Here is the prize I won
and bring you. For the winners in the minor events
were given horses to take away, while those who won   1030
the heavier stuff, boxing and wrestling, got oxen,
and a woman was thrown in with them. Since I happened
to be there, it seemed wrong to let this splendid prize
go by. As I said, the woman is for you to keep.
She is not stolen. It cost me hard work to bring   1035
her here. Some day, perhaps, you will say I have done well.

ADMETUS

I did not mean to dishonor nor belittle you
when I concealed the fate of my unhappy wife,
but it would have added pain to pain already there
if you had been driven to shelter with some other host.   1040
This sorrow is mine. It is enough for me to weep.
As for the woman, if it can be done, my lord,
I beg you, have some other Thessalian, who has not
suffered as I have, keep her. You have many friends
in Pherae. Do not bring my sorrows back to me.   1045
I would not have strength to see her in my house and keep
my eyes dry. I suffer now. Do not inflict further
suffering on me. I have sorrow enough to weigh me down.
And where could a young woman live in this house? For
she is young, I can see it in her dress, her style.   1050
Am I to put her in the same quarters with the men?
And how, circulating among young men, shall she be kept
from harm? Not easy, Heracles, to hold in check
a young strong man. I am thinking of your interests.
Or shall I put her in my lost wife's chamber, keep   1055
her there? How can I take her to Alcestis' bed?
I fear blame from two quarters, from my countrymen
who might accuse me of betraying her who helped
me most, by running to the bed of another girl,
and from the dead herself. Her honor has its claim   1060

on me. I must be very careful. You, lady,
whoever you are, I tell you that you have the same
form as my Alcestis; all your body is like hers.
Too much. Oh, by the gods, take this woman away
out of my sight. I am beaten already, do not beat   1065
me again. For as I look on her, I think I see
my wife. It churns my heart to tumult, and the tears
break streaming from my eyes. How much must I endure
the bitter taste of sorrow which is still so fresh?

CHORUS LEADER

I cannot put a good name to your fortune; yet   1070
whoever you are, you must endure what the god gives.

HERACLES

I only wish that my strength had been great enough
for me to bring your wife back from the chambered deep
into the light. I would have done that grace for you.

ADMETUS

I know you would have wanted to. Why speak of it?   1075
There is no way for the dead to come back to the light.

HERACLES

Then do not push your sorrow. Bear it as you must.

ADMETUS

Easier to comfort than to suffer and be strong.

HERACLES

But if you wish to mourn forever, what will you gain?

ADMETUS

Nothing. I know it. But some impulse of my love   1080
makes me.

HERACLES

Why, surely. Love for the dead is cause for tears.

ADMETUS

Her death destroyed me, even more than I can say.

HERACLES

You have lost a fine wife. Who will say you have not?

ADMETUS

So fine

that I, whom you see, never shall enjoy life again.

HERACLES

Time will soften the evil. It still is young and strong.   1085

ADMETUS

You can say time will soften it, if time means death.

HERACLES

A wife, your new marriage will put an end to this desire.

ADMETUS

Silence! I never thought you would say a thing like that.

HERACLES

What? You will not remarry but keep an empty bed?

ADMETUS

No woman ever shall sleep in my arms again.   1090

HERACLES

Do you believe you help the dead by doing this?

ADMETUS

Wherever she may be, she deserves my honors still.

HERACLES

Praiseworthy, yes, praiseworthy. And yet foolish, too.

ADMETUS

Call me so, then, but never call me a bridegroom.

HERACLES

I admire you for your faith and love you bear your wife.   1095

ADMETUS

Let me die if I betray her, though she is gone.

HERACLES

Well then,
receive this woman into your most generous house.

ADMETUS

Please, in the name of Zeus your father, no!

HERACLES

And yet
you will be making a mistake if you do not.

ADMETUS

And I'll be eaten at the heart with anguish if I do.   1100

HERACLES

Obey. The grace of this may come where you need grace.

ADMETUS

Ah.
I wish you had never won her in those games of yours.

HERACLES

Where I am winner, you are winner along with me.

ADMETUS

Honorably said. But let the woman go away.

HERACLES

She will go, if she should. First look. See if she should.   1105

ADMETUS

She should, unless it means you will be angry with me.

HERACLES

Something I know of makes me so insistent with you.

ADMETUS

So, win again. But what you do does not please me.

HERACLES

The time will come when you will thank me. Only obey.

ADMETUS   *(To attendants.)*

Escort her in, if she must be taken into this house.   1110

HERACLES

I will not hand this lady over to attendants.

ADMETUS

You yourself lead her into the house then, if you wish.

HERACLES

I will put her into your hands and into yours alone.

ADMETUS

I will not touch her. But she is free to come inside.

HERACLES

No, I have faith in your right hand, and only yours.   1115

ADMETUS

My lord, you are forcing me to act against my wish.

HERACLES

Be brave. Reach out your hand and touch the stranger.

ADMETUS

                                                          So.

Here is my hand; I feel like Perseus killing the Gorgon.

HERACLES

You have her?

ADMETUS

                    Yes, I have her.

HERACLES

                              Keep her, then. Some day

you will say the son of Zeus came as your generous guest.   1120

But look at her. See if she does not seem most like

your wife. Your grief is over now. Your luck is back.

ADMETUS

Gods, what shall I think! Amazement beyond hope, as I

look on this woman, this wife. Is she really mine,
or some sweet mockery for a god to stun me with? 1125

HERACLES

Not so. This is your own wife you see. She is here.

ADMETUS

Be careful she is not some phantom from the depths.

HERACLES

The guest and friend you took was no necromancer.

ADMETUS

Do I see my wife, whom I was laying in the grave?

HERACLES

Surely. But I do not wonder at your unbelief. 1130

ADMETUS

May I touch her, and speak to her, as my living wife?

HERACLES

Speak to her. All that you desired is yours.

ADMETUS

                                   Oh, eyes
and body of my dearest wife, I have you now
beyond all hope. I never thought I'd see you again.

HERACLES

You have her. May no god begrudge you your happiness. 1135

ADMETUS

O nobly sprung child of all-highest Zeus, may good
fortune go with you. May the father who gave you birth
keep you safe. You alone raised me up when I was down.
How did you bring her back from down there to the light?

HERACLES

I fought a certain deity who had charge of her. 1140

ADMETUS

Where do you say you fought this match with Death?

HERACLES

                                                            Beside

the tomb itself. I ambushed him and caught him in my
    hands.

ADMETUS

But why is my wife standing here, and does not speak?

HERACLES

You are not allowed to hear her speak to you until
    her obligations to the gods who live below   1145
    are washed away and the third morning comes. So now
    take her and lead her inside, and for the rest of time,
    Admetus, be just: treat your guests as they deserve.
    And now good-bye. I have my work that I must do,
    and go to face the lordly son of Sthenelus.   1150

ADMETUS

No, stay with us and be the guest of our hearth.

HERACLES

                                                    There still

will be a time for that, but I must press on now.

ADMETUS

Success go with you. May you find your way back here.

                                    (Exit Heracles to the side.)

I proclaim to all the people of my tetrarchy
    that, for these blessed happenings, they shall set up
    dances, and the altars smoke with sacrifice offered.   1155
    For now we shall make our life again, and it will be
    a better one.
                    I was lucky. That I cannot deny.

                            (Exit with Alcestis into the house.)

CHORUS [chanting]
    Many are the forms of what is divine.

Much that the gods achieve is surprise.   1160
What we look for does not come to pass;
a god finds a way for what none foresaw.
Such was the end of this story.

(Exit all.)

TEXTUAL NOTES

(The line numbers indicated are in some cases only approximate.)

THE EUMENIDES

85-87. Some scholars transpose these lines to before line 64.

104-5. Most editors delete line 104 ("Eyes . . . brain"); some delete 105 as well.

188. The exact reading and translation are uncertain; but the general sense is not in doubt.

352. One line appears to be missing after this.

360-61. The text and meaning of these two lines are very uncertain.

381. Some editors adopt here the emendation, "For we alone" (*monai*), instead of the manuscript's "all holds" (*menei*).

404. After this line, the manuscripts contain a line that says, "after yoking this chariot of mine to speedy horses." Editors delete this as it contradicts the previous two lines. Presumably the line was inserted for an alternative mode of entry to the stage for Athena in a later production.

435. The precise reading here is uncertain.

491. The manuscripts here read "overthrow of new laws." Most editors have adopted some kind of emendation, since "new" appears to mean the opposite of what is required by the context. In the first edition, Lattimore translated as "overthrow of all the young laws."

565. Scholars disagree as to whether Athena appoints eleven or twelve human jurors. Since in the end her vote is counted along with theirs and the total of votes is then equal (711-53), it appears that they should be an odd number.

632-33. Some scholars have suggested that a line may be missing here.

775-77. Some scholars assign these lines to Apollo rather than to Orestes.

932. Text uncertain.

1027. Some lines may be missing here. Perhaps in them the Erinyes were called "Eumenides" (the name, which gives this play its title, does not occur anywhere in the extant text).

PHILOCTETES

177. The manuscripts read, "Oh hands of mortals," but both meter and sense seem to require this emendation.

204. The manuscripts assign this one line (improbably) to Neoptolemus.

217. Some editors interpret differently, "perhaps he saw no ship in the unfriendly harbor."

361. An alternative reading gives, "I came to the Atridae in a friendly manner."

385-88. Some modern editors regard these lines as an interpolation.

452. Some editors emend to read, "in surveying divine activities, I find the gods are bad."

852-54. The precise reading and interpretation of these lines are uncertain.

1140. Text uncertain. Some editors read, "A man should take heed to say what is just."

1153. The text translated here is an emendation of the manuscripts' reading, "The place is slackly guarded, and need not be feared."

1218-21. Some editors delete these lines as an interpolation.

1251-52. A line or two may have dropped out here.

1361. Precise text and interpretation uncertain.

1365. The manuscripts contain one extra line here, which all modern editors omit: "They judged wretched Ajax second to Odysseus in the award of your father's weapons."

1395. This is the reading of most of the manuscripts. Some editors adopt a simple emendation which gives, "It is time now to leave my argument . . ."

1407-8. The text of these two lines is uncertain; some words are missing in the manuscripts.

1408. Heracles' role is played by the same actor who played both Odysseus and the Sailor/Merchant. Some modern critics have suggested that the audience is meant to think that this is Odysseus, in disguise, but it seems unlikely that Sophocles would have provided no clue anywhere in the text to such a significant impersonation. Heracles' voice might nonetheless have sounded somewhat similar to Odysseus', and some spectators might well have wondered if this was really Heracles they were hearing.

OEDIPUS AT COLONUS

3. More exactly, "this day."

8. More accurately, "nobility."

49-50. Or more literally, "By the gods, stranger, do not dishonor a wanderer such as I am, by refusing to tell me what I ask."

95. More exactly, "the bright flash of Zeus."

97. Or, "with trustworthy omens."

103. More exactly, "according to the sacred utterances of Apollo."

127-28. More literally, "into the inviolate grove of these dreadful Maidens," that is, the Furies.

164. Some editors emend to read "Let there be a greater distance from there."

171. More exactly, "Father, we should pay attention to the townsmen."

183. About four lyric lines appear to be missing before this, since the corresponding antistrophe has several more phrases than the strophe here.

212. More exactly, "My birth and nature are dreadful."

235-37. Or more exactly, "Depart quickly from my land, lest you bring some further trouble to my city!"

248. More literally, "Grant your unexpected approval!"

253. More accurately, "You will never see a mortal man who, if a god leads, can escape."

279-80. More exactly, "upon the mortal who is reverent, and upon the irreverent too."

287-90. More accurately, "I come here sacred and reverent, and I bring advantage to this race, as you may learn more fully when the man with authority comes, whoever is your leader."

325. Or "sweetest names to utter!"

327. Text uncertain: the manuscripts have "unfortunate," but the emendation "old and worn" is preferred by many editors.

371. More exactly, "some god" and "their own evil/sinful mind."

378. More exactly, "has gone to Argos . . . as an exile."

380-81. The text is uncertain here. Many editors adopt a simple emendation, so that instead of "Argos shall . . . win . . . ," Polynices is telling them that "he himself shall . . . win Thebes . . . or else go up to heaven."

406. More exactly, "Will they cover my body with Theban dust?"

450. More exactly, "They will never win me as their ally."

508-9. More literally, "For parents, not even if one labors should it be thought of as labor."

527-28. More exactly, "Was it with your mother, as I hear, that you shared your ill-famed bed?"

539-40. More literally, "I received a gift, which I wish I had never accepted, for having given help."

547. Text uncertain. Some editors emend to read "I was captured by doom; I killed . . ."

579. More accurately, "What profit do you claim to bring?"

587. More exactly, "The contest is no small one."

590. More accurately, "But if you wish that, it is not good for you to remain in exile."

606. More literally, "And how would my affairs and theirs become bitter?"

658-60. Many scholars have rejected these lines as a post-Sophoclean interpolation.

669-71. More exactly, "*you have come, guest, to Colonus . . . and you shall not seek another home.*"

685-87. More literally, "*the river's fountains are awake, Cephisus' nomadic streams that run unthinned forever, and never stay . . .*"

695-98. More precisely, "*And our land has a thing unknown in Asia's vast terrain or in the Dorian isle to our west where Pelops' race holds sway.*"

718-19. Or, a little more exactly, *"following the hundred-footed Nereids and their dance."*

735-36. More exactly, "I, despite my age, am sent to persuade him to follow me back to Thebes."

756-57. Text uncertain.

848. Literally, "Oh wretched, wretched am I!"

861-62. In the manuscripts, both these lines are spoken by Creon, and the reading is "It will be done, unless the ruler of this land prevents me!" Several modern editors have emended the second line so as to read "you," as here, and have assigned this line to the chorus.

882. A few words in the chorus' reply seem to be missing here.

942. More literally, "my relatives."

945. The reading is uncertain. The text in the manuscripts seems to refer to "someone with whom children from an unholy marriage are living."

954-55. Some editors regard these two lines as an interpolation.

964-65. More exactly, "It was the gods' pleasure, and perhaps our family had angered them long ago."

975-76. More exactly, "and killed him, not knowing what I was doing, nor whom I was doing it to."

1007-8. More literally, "me, an old man and a suppliant . . ."

1033. Some editors transpose lines 1028-33 to follow 1019.

1043. More literally, "and may you benefit from your righteous concern for us!"

1044-95. Robert Fitzgerald's version of this choral song is composed as a sequence of rhyming stanzas and refrains, and it is somewhat freer as a translation of Sophocles' Greek than his rendering of the other choral songs of the play. A less poetic, but more exact, version of the first strophe and antistrophe might be the following:

STROPHE A
Oh, to be where the enemies wheel about,
to hear the shout and brazen sound of war!   1045
Or maybe on Apollo's sacred shore,
or by that torchlit Eleusinian plain

where pilgrims come, so that
the Great Ladies may provide solemn rites
for those mortals on whose tongues the golden key   1050
of the sweet-voiced Ministers rests.
For even to those regions the warrior king Theseus
will press the fighting on—as he brings
help to the two maiden sisters,   1055
self-sufficient in his battle-strength!

ANTISTROPHE A

Perhaps they are approaching now the plain
west of snowy mount Oea,   1060
if they are fleeing on horses
or on swift-racing chariots;
yet they'll be taken: for fearsome is the spirit   1065
of the local people, and fearsome Theseus's army;
the harnesses flash like mountain lightning.
These are the riders of Athens, conquered never;
they honor her whose glory all men know,   1070
and honor Poseidon too, son of Rhea and god of the sea,
the one who holds the earth firm.

1067–69. Text uncertain.

1080. More exactly, "I can prophesy a good outcome to this contest!"

1094–95. More exactly, "so that both of you come to lend your help to this land and its citizens."

1116. More accurately, "for girls so young."

1118. The precise text is uncertain here, but the general sense seems clear.

1158. More literally, "sitting as a suppliant at Poseidon's altar."

1166. More exactly, "would come here to make this supplication?"

1202–3. Or, more exactly, "and you, who are yourself being well treated, should know how to pay proper return for such treatment."

1210. More exactly, "you are safe, if one of the gods will keep my life safe too."

1268. More exactly, "of Zeus."

1278. More literally, "I am a suppliant of the god."

1300. This line is rejected by some editors as an interpolation.

1341. More literally, "scattering him."

1357. More exactly, "clad in these rags that now you are weeping about."

1370. More exactly, "And so it is that a god is watching you."

1373. Literally, "polluted by blood."

1382. More accurately, "of Zeus."

1410. More literally, "proper funeral rites."

1436. Some editors reject this line as an interpolation.

1463. More exactly, "Look there!"

1470. After this line, the manuscripts contain several more lines, which Robert Fitzgerald originally translated as follows:

CHORUS [singing]
    Ah, Zeus! Majestic heaven!

OEDIPUS
    My children, the appointed end has come;
    I can no longer turn away from it.

ANTIGONE
    How do you know? What is the sign that tells you?

OEDIPUS
    I know it clearly now. Let someone quickly   1475
    send for the king and bring him here to me!
                            (Thunder and lightning.)

1477. In the manuscripts, this choral stanza begins, "*Ah, ah, see once more!*"

1482–84. Or more exactly:

    May I find you favorably disposed,
    and though I have looked on an accursed man,
    may I not be paid back to my loss!

1498. More exactly, "*as just repayment to you and the city and his dear ones for what he has endured.*"

1511–13. The manuscripts here contain three lines which Robert Fitzgerald does not translate:

OEDIPUS
    The gods themselves as heralds proclaim to me
    with no deception; the signs are plain and true.

THESEUS
What do you mean? How are these things revealed?

1531–3. More literally:

> then you must tell it
> only to the foremost citizen, and he in turn
> must teach it to his successor, and so forever.

1559–60. More literally, "*pray to you, Aidoneus, king of the regions of night.*"

1570. More exactly, "*the invincible beast Cerberus, growling at the gate of the all-welcoming hosts.*"

1615. More literally, "*And yet one word dissolves all those hardships.*"

1640. The exact text is uncertain but the meaning is clear.

1661. More exactly, "*But either some escort sent from the gods . . .*"

1717. Some words have apparently dropped out here, since the antistrophe is two lines shorter than the corresponding strophe.

1746. More literally, "*A wide sea of troubles it is for you.*" This line is followed in the manuscripts by Antigone singing "Yes, yes" and the chorus "I agree too." Some scholars reject these phrases as an interpolation.

1751–53. The manuscripts attribute these lines to the Chorus Leader, but modern scholars assign them to Theseus.

1767. More exactly, "*and the god heard me, and so did Oath, the son of Zeus, who hears everything.*"

1779. More literally, "*Altogether, these things have their appointed end.*"

THE BACCHAE

72–82. Euripides' language here employs some traditional elements of ceremonial Greek "blessing" (*makarismos*), and William Arrowsmith's original translation of these lines used Christian language, especially from the Beatitudes in the (King James) Authorized Version of the New Testament, to convey something of the sacral fervor of the chorus:

> —Blessèd, blessèd are those who know the mysteries of god.
> —Blessèd is he who hallows his life in the worship of god,
>   he whom the spirit of god possesseth, who is one
>   with those who belong to the holy body of god.   75
> —Blessèd are the dancers and those who are purified,

who dance on the hill in the holy dance of god.
—Blessèd are they who keep the rite of Cybele the Mother.
—Blessèd are the thyrsus-bearers, those who wield in their hands
the holy wand of god.   80
—Blessèd are those who wear the crown of the ivy of god.
—Blessèd, blessèd are they: Dionysus is their god!

151. The text of this line is uncertain.

182. This line is similar to line 860 and is rejected by some scholars as an interpolation here.

200. Some scholars assign this line to Cadmus. Possibly one line may have dropped out after it.

315. Text uncertain.

316. This line is identical to *Hippolytus* 80 and is rejected by many scholars here as an interpolation.

428-29. The text of these lines is uncertain, though their sense is clear.

506. The text of these words is suspect.

540. Before this line the manuscripts transmit the words "What fury, what fury!"; they are rejected by most modern scholars as an ungrammatical interpolation.

585. This word is missing in the manuscripts and is supplied by modern scholars.

606. The text of the last part of this line is uncertain.

631. This word is missing in the manuscripts and is supplied by modern scholars.

652. A line has almost certainly been lost in the manuscript, most likely containing Dionysus' reply to Pentheus' disparagement of the god in line 652; on this assumption, the words "The god himself will come to teach you wisdom" give one possible indication of what might have been lost. But some scholars instead assign line 652 to Dionysus and suggest that the line that has been lost was the previous one, containing Pentheus' retort in response to Dionysus' praise of the god in line 651.

673. This line is similar to one transmitted as part of a quotation from a lost play of Euripides and is rejected here by some scholars as an interpolation.

716. This line is similar to line 667 and is rejected here by many scholars as an interpolation.

757. This sentence seems out of place here and is transposed by many scholars, with some changes, to follow after line 761.

842. Two half lines seem to have been lost here.

877. Text and meaning of this line are uncertain.

896. Text and meaning of this line are uncertain.

973-76. Either Pentheus exits before these lines and does not hear them; or else he is still on stage but is so dazed that he does not seem to hear or understand them. Given that Dionysus leads him throughout this whole episode, the latter alternative seems likelier.

996-1010. Arrowsmith's original translation of this antistrophe elaborates freely upon the themes suggested by the very uncertain and difficult Greek text:

—Uncontrollable, the unbeliever goes,
  in spitting rage, rebellious and amok,
  madly assaulting the mysteries of god,
  profaning the rites of the mother of god.
  Against the unassailable he runs, with rage   1000
  obsessed. Headlong he runs to death.
  For death the gods exact, curbing by that bit
  the mouths of men. They humble us with death
  that we remember what we are who are not god,
  but men. We run to death. Wherefore, I say,
  accept, accept:
  humility is wise; humility is blest.
  But what the world calls wise I do not want.   1005
  Elsewhere the chase. I hunt another game,
  those great, those manifest, those certain goals,
  achieving which, our mortal lives are blest.
  Let these things be the quarry of my chase:
  purity; humility; an unrebellious soul,
  accepting all. Let me go the customary way,
  the timeless, honored, beaten path of those who walk
  with reverence and awe beneath the sons of heaven.   1010

1002-7. The meter and meaning of these lines are very uncertain.

1025-26. These lines are rejected by some scholars as an interpolation.

1028. This line is similar to *Medea* 54 and is rejected by many scholars here as an interpolation.

1036. The rest of this line and probably one more following line are missing in the manuscript.

1060. The translation reflects the text of the manuscript; many editors accept a modern scholarly emendation that yields the sense, "I cannot see their frantic illnesses."

1090. After this line the medieval manuscript has two lines that are missing in an ancient papyrus and that are rejected by modern scholars: "running with intense runnings of the feet, mother Agave and her kindred sisters."

1158. The text of these last words is uncertain.

1174. Most of a line is missing here.

1221. After this line the manuscript transmits a line that has been omitted here: "having picked them up where they were lying in a forest difficult to search."

1244-45. One or both of these lines are rejected by many scholars as an interpolation.

1301. At least one line containing Cadmus' reply to Agave, and probably rather more, has been lost here.

1329. Scholars use the following sources to reconstruct the missing section of the play: (1) one of the hypotheses (ancient scholarly summaries) of the play, according to which "Dionysus appeared and then addressed all of them and revealed to each one what would happen to him or her" (there follow some corrupt words); (2) Apsines, a third-century CE rhetorician, who writes, "In Euripides, Pentheus' mother Agave is freed from her madness and recognizes her son who has been torn apart; then she accuses herself and arouses pity.... Euripides deploys this rhetorical device because he wishes to arouse commiseration for Pentheus: the mother takes up each of his limbs in her hands and laments each one in turn"; (3) *Christus Patiens* (*The Passion of Christ*), an anonymous Byzantine cento (a poetic text consisting entirely of citations from famous works by earlier poets) which is probably to be dated to the twelfth century, and containing a number of lines that have been attributed with more or less probability to this play (especially lines 1011, 1120-23, 1256-57, 1312-13, 1449, and 1466-72 for Agave's speech; and 300, 1360-62, 1639-40, 1663-1679, 1690, and 1756 for Dionysus'); (4) a line quoted from the scholia (ancient commentary) on line 907 of Aristophanes' *Wealth* as coming from this play; and (5) a few very scrappy papyrus fragments.

1344, 1346, 1348. Some scholars assign these lines to Agave.

1351. It is not certain, but most likely, that Dionysus exits at this point. But see note on lines 1377-78.

1353. This word is missing in the manuscript and has been restored by modern scholars.

1372. After this line a line is missing containing the rest of Cadmus' reply to Agave; the words "burial place . . . son on Cithaeron" give one possible indication of what has been lost.

1374-76. Text uncertain.

1377-78. The manuscript assigns these lines to Dionysus (who in that case did not exit after line 1351) and reads, "I was terribly blasphemed by you, / my name dishonored in Thebes"; the translation reflects a widely accepted modern scholarly emendation.

1385. Text uncertain.

1388-92. These lines are rejected by many scholars as non-Euripidean.

ALCESTIS

Characters. The list of characters prefixed to the play in the manuscripts identifies the boy's name as Eumelus, but there is nothing to support this in the play itself and it is probably just an ancient scholarly guess. In Homer's *Iliad* Eumelus is the son of Admetus and Alcestis.

16. Many scholars reject this line as an interpolation.

77. The manuscripts indicate that different members of the chorus chant or sing the various sections of the following entrance song; editors differ on the exact distribution.

93-94. Text uncertain.

207-8. These two lines are identical to *Hecuba* 411-12 and are probably an interpolation here.

211. Many editors divide the chorus here into groups and distribute the various sections of this song to different groups.

215. Text uncertain.

312. The manuscripts add here the line, "He can talk with him and be spoken to in turn." This is rejected by most scholars as an interpolation (cf. 195).

393. See note on Characters above.

411. About a line of text is missing here.

458. This line is rejected by some scholars; if it is retained, then a line must be missing before 469 (in the antistrophe).

469. See on line 458 (in the strophe).

603. The manuscripts are punctuated to read, "*All of wisdom is there in the noble. I stand in awe, and good hope . . .*" The translation reflects a modern re-punctuation.

651-52. These two lines are almost identical to 295-96 and are rejected here by most scholars as an interpolation.

708. Some manuscripts read not "have spoken" but "am speaking."

795-96. The words "put flowers on your head" and "fight down these present troubles" are repeated in the Greek text in lines 829 and 832, and are probably an interpolation here.

818-19. These two lines are said by ancient commentators to have been missing in some manuscripts, and are rejected by most modern scholars.

CPSIA information can be obtained
at www.ICGtesting.com
Printed in the USA
LVOW10s1218170118
562864LV00002B/2/P

9 780226 035932